STEEL/CITY

STEEL/CITY

A DOCUDRAMA IN THREE ACTS

Gillette Elvgren and Attilio Favorini

University of Pittsburgh Press

Pittsburgh and London

Published by the University of Pittsburgh Press, Pittsburgh, Pa., 15260
Copyright © 1976, 1992, Gillette Elvgren and Attilio Favorini
All rights reserved
Eurospan, London
Manufactured in the United States of America
Printed on acid-free paper

Library of Congress Cataloging-in-Publication Data

Elvgren, Gillette.
   Steel/City : a docudrama in three acts / Gillette Elvgren and Attilio Favorini.
     p. cm.
   Contents: Includes bibliographical references (p.   ).
   ISBN 0-8229-3707-7 (cl). — ISBN 0-8229-5470-2 (pb)
   1. Steel industry and trade—Pennsylvania—Pittsburgh Region—History—Drama. 2. Pittsburgh (Pa.)—History—Drama.
I. Favorini, Attilio, 1943- . II. Title.
PS3555.L83S74   1992
812 '.54—dc20   91-50874
                                                                                                                             CIP

A CIP catalogue record for this book is available from the British Library.

Caution: Professionals and amateurs are hereby warned that *Steel/City*, being fully protected under the copyright laws of the United States of America, the British Empire, including the Dominion of Canada, and all other countries of the Universal Copyright and Berne Conventions, is subject to royalty. All rights, including professional, amateur, motional picture, recitation, lecturing, public reading, radio and television broadcasting, and the rights of translation into foreign languages, are strictly reserved. Particular emphasis is given to readings, permission for which must be secured in writing. All inquiries should be addressed to Attilio Favorini, c/o the University of Pittsburgh Press, 127 N. Bellefield Ave., Pittsburgh PA 15260.

Contents

Acknowledgments   vii

Documentary Theater
and the Historian's Art   ix

Steel/City   3

Note on Sources   105

Acknowledgments

We would like to thank the following institutions and individuals for their assistance in the research for *Steel/City*: the Archives of Industrial Society and the Curtis Theatre Collection of Hillman Library, the Frick Fine Arts Library, the Darlington Collection—all at the University of Pittsburgh; the Western Pennsylvania Historical Society; the Pennsylvania State University Library system; the Pennsylvania Historical and Museum Commission; the library of the United States Steel Corporation; Jan Stewart, Susan Jacobelli, Toby Beckwith, Larry Meyers, John Gregurich, George M. Jones, Jacob Evanson, Karen Byrne, Susan Stern, Joseph A. Jacobelli, Colletta Henry, and Elaine Herdtfelder.

The following individuals agreed to share with us their oral histories: Katherine Pellegrino, Kay Kluz, Joseph Odorcich, Lefty Scumaci, Wayne Alderson, Tony Zema, Walter Klis, Philomena Klis, Mary Mushalko, Don Mushalko, Mary Magdic, John Magdic, Mike Stosik, Sam Davich, William Adomitas, Steve Pavacic, D. P. Cromwell, Anthony Desena, Antoinette Shanofski, Paul Jakiela, and Mike Zahorsky.

Lynda Kaiserman indefatigably typed the original script of the play; Rick Whitten typed the complete manuscript for publication. Ellen Kelson rechecked our sources, as did our editor Jane Flanders. We thank them all for their generous and expert service. Finally, we gratefully acknowledge the support of our families, whose enthusiasm fired the furnace that made the play.

Documentary Theater and the Historian's Art

Documentary Theater in the Twentieth Century

Steel/City is a documentary drama (with music) memorializing the history of the steel industry in Pittsburgh and its environs. It received both amateur and professional production at the University of Pittsburgh in 1976, toured the steel towns of the Monongahela Valley on a performance barge, and played at the Smithsonian Institution's Festival of American Folklife in August of that Bicentennial year. To our delight, the play had broad-based appeal, as local workers and their families with names like Davich and Kluz, Zahorsky and Magdic came to the theater for the first time to see the story of their city and their clans represented through music and spectacle, and especially to hear their own stories told by actors—word for word.

Documentary theater has taken different forms in this century, drawing on a variety of theatrical idioms and techniques: choruses, narrators, slide projections, mime, naturalistic and expressionistic elements—some or all of which may be found in any given example of the type. Such tight and controlled works as Peter Weiss's *The Investigation* (1965) and Heinar Kipphardt's *In the Matter of J. Robert Oppenheimer* (1964), which use government documents and court proceedings exclusively, are no more or less typical than the theatrical clown show of Joan Littlewood's *Oh, What a Lovely War!* (1963) or the militant Chicanismo of Luis Valdez's *Zoot Suit* (1978). But in its reliance on actual rather than invented event, on dialogue "found" in the historical record or gathered by the playwright/researcher, and in its disposition to set individual behavior in an articulated political and social environment, documentary drama may be studied as a discrete development in twentieth-century theater. Furthermore, in opposition to an absurdist point of view, "the documentary theater affirms that reality, whatever the obscurity in which it masks itself, can be explained in minute detail."[1] A positivist position of this sort, of course, is even more controversial now than when thus affirmed by Peter Weiss in 1968, and we shall take up the controversy later in this essay.

Documentary theater, like documentary film, originated during the First World War. In retrospect, the edited World War I footage taken by the British Film Board and used to inform the general public about the progress of the war may be identified as the first film documentaries, although the term is not recorded prior to John Grierson's 1926 usage in reference to Robert Flaherty's film *Moana*. It is not easy to draw a line between the newsreel and the documentary from this period, particularly in light of intermediate formats like *Captain Scott's Expedition to the South Pole* (1912) and *Battle of the Somme* (1916). In any case, with its connotation of "evidence" and its implication of veracity, the term soon became useful in identifying art works aspiring to historical and political "truth."[2]

Documentary theater's origins are likewise "to be found in the years following the First World War. Before 1914 drama (and life?) was largely conceived of as 'character in action.' But the cataclysm of the Great War and the social collapse of a supposedly stable Europe made artists aware that there were greater forces at work in society than the clash of personalities. Dramatic emphasis shifted from the character to the event."[3] While the genre may therefore be seen as a rejection of psychological drama in the realistic idiom which came to dominate European theater in the late nineteenth century, it is at the same time an heir to naturalism. For documentary theater is an alternative response by the theater artist to Comte, Marx, Darwin, and Spencer, who examined individual behavior in a context bound by social, economic, and physical laws. In embracing the nineteenth-century scientific model of truth as fact supported by empirical evidence, documentary theater accepts for itself an odd, hybrid status, as its mimesis finds its sources partly outside the theatrical realm, in the arena of pragmatics. Aristotle would have probably considered it monstrous.

The documentary theater quickly became a medium for the political expression of the vast social upheaval and unrest that followed the war. After the Russian Revolution, "spoken newspaper" pieces were designed to inform workers, peasants, and Red Army soldiers of the progress of the civil war. Verhaeren's *Dawns* (1920), for example, incorporated nightly news reports from the front. In the late 1920s German leftists adopted documentary theater techniques in the hopes of politicizing the discontented masses and combating the rise of the Right—Erwin Piscator's use of filmed sequences in the antiwar *Good Soldier Schweik* (1928) being an important example.

Piscator is prominently associated with the development of "epic theater," whose aims and techniques overlap documentary theater without accepting its restriction of found dialogue. In a tribute to Piscator, the documentary playwright Kipphardt acknowledged their common belief that "the theatre must be objective on the basis of a materialistic conception of history."[4] Piscator's plea was for a theater that related historic events and revealed fundamentally true political and social relationships. In such a work as *In Spite of Everything* (1925), which dealt with the fate of Rosa Luxemburg and Karl Liebknecht after the aborted revolution of 1918, Piscator's intention was to create drama based on the principles of news reportage, constructed in an epic succession of tableaux and stations, and designed to promote direct social action. It was in reference to Piscator's epic theater that Bertolt Brecht used the term *documentary* in 1926, the same year Grierson applied the term to Flaherty's film.[5]

Piscator's development of epic documentary theater had a pronounced influence on a similar but slightly later movement in the United States. The Depression, and the economic exploitation and suffering that it created, saw the inception of a novel government experiment, the Federal Theater Project. Established in 1935 under the leadership of Hallie Flanagan Davis, the project employed thousands of theater workers and developed and produced hundreds of new and classic plays throughout the country. Perhaps the most prominent and controversial of its activities was the creation of the Living Newspaper, so called because much of the dialogue for these pieces was taken directly from news media sources and government documents. The Living Newspaper borrowed heavily not only from the epic scene progression developed by Piscator and his associate Bertolt Brecht, but also from the technical innovations Piscator advocated—multilevel sets, projections, loudspeakers, and an ironic juxtaposition of live stage image with cool and objective projected image.

The Living Newspaper usually entailed the dramatization of a problem—"composed in greater or lesser extent of many news events, all bearing on the one subject and interlarded with typical but nonfactual representations of the effect of these news events on the people to whom the problem is of great importance."[6] Topics such as the political decisions that created the Tennessee Valley Authority (*Power*, 1937), slum housing (*One-Third of a Nation*, 1938), and venereal disease (*Spirochete*, 1938) typify the content of these docudramas.

In four short years, the Federal Theater Project was itself history, an early victim of the House Un-American Activities Committee. Because of their undisguised liberal bias, the Living Newspapers had been an especially easy target for those charged with investigating "un-American propaganda activities" and "Communist leanings." From the very beginning, the FTP encountered political obstacles. Elmer Rice's *Ethiopia* (1935), a Living Newspaper production on the Ethiopian War, was never permitted to open, and Paul Peters's and George Sklar's *Stevedore* was banned in several locations. Opposition was nationwide. According to John O'Connor and Lorraine Brown, "Though each region was encouraged to develop living newspapers on local problems, few were produced. The national office of the FTP wanted full documentation and proof they were factually accurate," no doubt responding to political pressure.[7]

Most of the early British attempts at documentary theater were directly influenced by the Living Newspaper. The Merseyside Unity Theatre in London was the gathering place for advocates of documentary theater before World War II. During the 1930s such works as *Busmen*, which dealt with a strike of London bus drivers, and the poetic pageant *Stay Down Miner* were the most notable documentary fare. After the war the Theatre Workshop created and produced *Uranium 235*, which treated in documentary format the events culminating in the detonation of the first atomic bomb. The production remained in their repertory for several years. In 1946 the Reunion Theatre, an organization of demobilized servicemen, produced *Exercise Bowler*, which dealt literally and figuratively with the problem of substituting the bowler hat for the service cap. The play was popular enough to be transferred to London's West End.

But it was left to Joan Littlewood and her brilliant and savagely satirical *Oh, What a Lovely War!* to touch off a whole new interest in documentary theater in England. Charles Marowitz, an American director residing in London, described the 19 March 1963 premiere at the Theatre Royal:

xiv / Introduction

> A panoramic view of the pathos and absurdity of the Kaiser's War, the production is a medley of disparate styles which the genius of Littlewood and the invention of the ensemble have welded into one. The music-hall score which accurately conveys the lace-trimmed romanticism of the early 1900's is interpolated with the brash journalistic devices of a Living Newspaper—creating an effect which is at once epic and intimate; elegantly stylized and grimly realistic; tragic and tragic-comic.[8]

Oh, What a Lovely War! does not pretend to present both sides of the question. It is resolutely, uncompromisingly, "unfairly" antiwar, though there is no lecturing, no sentimentality, no overt didacticism. Rather, the satiric blending of improvised scenes, slide projections, and especially songs make the most devastating comment. The performers are a cast of Pierrot clowns, changing hats, props, and characters with equal facility—while never letting the audience relax into forgetful laughter. As characters are killed off only to rise again, clown smiles pasted in place, ready to die once more, the impact of this stage metaphor becomes crushing—ultimately forcing the audience to look through all the false romanticism and gushing, tearful patriotism at the face of war.

Oh, What a Lovely War! began a remarkable resurgence of documentary theater in England. Peter Cheeseman, the articulate and energetic director of a small professional repertory company in the Midlands called the Victoria, saw Littlewood's production in 1964. He immediately started work on a musical documentary of his own entitled *The Jolly Potters* which told the history of the potteries industry in Stoke-on-Trent and the Five Towns, an area noted for its exquisite Royal Doulton, Wedgewood, and Spode china. Its initial success generated yearly docudramas at the Victoria dealing with such topics as the history of the local rail line (*The Knotty*), the federation of the Six Towns (*Six Into One*), the life of Hugh Bourne, the founder of Primitive Methodism (*The Burning Mountain*), the history of Staffordshire during the English Civil War (*The Staffordshire Rebels*), and many more.

In 1971–1972 Gillette Elvgren spent close to a year in Stoke studying Peter Cheeseman's approach to documentary drama, its relationship to the community, and its realization through theater-in-the-round staging at the Victoria. Thus Cheeseman's artfully acticulated methods and rationale had a profound influence on the Elvgren/Favorini script of *Steel/City*, as well as on its mounting at the University of Pittsburgh in 1976. Because of this influence and because Cheeseman's doctrinaire defense of documentary theater as theater-of-fact raises intriguing theoretical questions, Cheeseman's work at the Victoria invites more detailed attention.

Documentary Drama as Theater-of-Fact

Peter Cheeseman's requisites for documentary theater are that it maintain "objectivity," that it be based in and authenticated by the exclusive use of primary source materials, and that it eschew propaganda. Clearly, in this insistence on objectivity Cheeseman was bucking the main current of documentary theater in the 1960s and 1970s. In "14 Propositions for a Documentary Theatre," Peter Weiss—while staking out a positivist position on historical fact—demands that documentary theater take sides: through the caricature of both personalities and situations, and by means of stylized gestures and masks, a certain historical moment can be molded to fit the author's particular ideology.[9] Similarly, although Heinar Kipphardt constructed *In the Matter of J. Robert Oppenheimer* entirely of factual material, both he and his director Piscator manipulated the data to support their own political and social agenda.

The mainstream of documentary theater during the 1960s was German. Its source may be traced to Schiller, who believed the theater to be a moral institution that should function like the pulpit or podium. This moral emphasis has become traditional. According to A. V. Subiotto, the theater in Germany "has long fulfilled the function of a tribune or rostrum."[10] Moreover, a specific event in the early sixties—the televised and stage-managed trial of Adolf Eichmann in 1961, both in its form (court setting, presentation of evidence, etcetera) and content (historical accuracy, moral accountability, political responsibility)—inspired a generation of German writers who revived the documentary dramatic idiom in the 1960s.[11]

By contrast, Peter Cheeseman is so leery of the encroachment of ideology that he enjoins playwrights not to "write" the play, but merely to do research and to cull dramatic material from interviews and written sources. As well, Cheeseman's actors have themselves often conducted library research and have tape-recorded oral histories to be used in production. Cheeseman is not naive enough to suggest that the inevitable arrangement, editing, and abridgement do not involve subjectivity and personal judgment, but he does intend that the compositional pains taken by his company should innoculate his productions against political narrow-mindedness and partisanship. As he says,

> I believe in the power of the artist, but I believe his job is something that is important in itself. The important part of the artist's credentials is that he should be completely independent. He must be free from any association with a formal political alignment, otherwise he has lost his credence. We have to find a way of asking disturbing questions which do not take a single viewpoint or single political alignment.[12]

Cheeseman is concerned with creating an audience of listeners rather than an audience of believers:

One of the things wrong with our society is that too few people have a sense of history. We have lost in our society the sort of natural structure whereby old men pass down knowledge to the young in a community; and people are not taught history intelligently. In this sort of atmosphere it seems to me that our obligation is to show people the past of their community in a way which will give them a sense of their past, in the knowledge that they not stand alone in the present but are part of a historical perspective.[13]

Cheeseman measures documentary theater by the "purity" of its representation of factual material: "The sensation of watching a documentary is the sensation of watching a fact. You can't write a documentary—it's a contradiction in terms. You can only edit documentary material."[14] The aesthetic nature of the theater event, however, as well as the convention of impersonation itself pose special challenges to a producer with such convictions: as soon as the actor walks on the stage, everyone in the audience knows he is a liar. Therefore, Cheeseman has had to develop a variety of production techniques to authenticate his productions, though without extinguishing the imaginative force of live theater.

Cannily undermining the distinction between professional actor and member of the community, Peter Cheeseman typically insists that his actors, who come from all over England, steep themselves in the Midlands accent, even arranging to have them live with local residents. They are taken to rail yards (*The Knotty*) and steel mills (*Fight for Shelton Bar*) to study the motions, the breathing, the rhythms of work. Following Brecht, the actors' dialogue is often cast in the third person—" 'Get me out a 'ere,' he said." Song and dance numbers help to move the play through difficult time and place transitions. Actor-narrators quote their sources, and taped voices of the real people interviewed are played during the production as voice-over, with actors assuming the voice and playing the scene.

Most docudramas use photo projections to provide visual variety and to convey factual data graphically. Since it is both technically difficult and expensive to include projections in theater-in-the-round performances, Cheeseman puts special emphasis on the actor as the direct visual representation of the documentary fact. The actor, he says, "must have a totally candid and honest basic relationship with the audience to start with."[15] Cheeseman believes there is a point when the verisimilitude of portrayal begins to pull the audience away from attending to the documentary material. He maintains the audience's objectivity by having any one actor play several different roles and by having their transformations, as they move from character to character, occur in full sight of the audience.

By excluding all fictional sources, Cheeseman runs the risk of sacrificing art to credibility, since even the most imaginative staging cannot bring to life a tedious bit of text. As one of Cheeseman's contemporaries observes, "The main risk of the documentary theatre . . . stems from the great distance between it and the other theatre—for in practice it is 'something else,' but it runs the risk that this 'something else' may not be art."[16] Cheeseman is concerned that his documentaries should be art, while admitting disarmingly that they may not be great art: "They're not meant to be great art at all. They are in fact occasional and circumstantial shows made for our home theater each year and have only accidental meaning and purpose outside that situation."[17]

Nevertheless, Cheeseman himself would probably admit that at the very basis of every good documentary is a sense that the issues covered go beyond a narrow parochialism. *The Knotty*, for example, could hardly be more specific to Stoke-on-Trent, but it is also a look at the struggle of any small town to define its identity in the face of burgeoning industrialism.

Documentaries have had a crucial impact on Cheeseman's theater in Stoke-on-Trent. They have identified the theater with the history of the community and its present concerns, created new audiences drawn from the working class, helped to erase the elitist image of the theater, and, at times, made theater as necessary to the community as the grocer or the baker. Perhaps the most striking example of a documentary establishing a virtual intertextuality with the community is the 1973 production of *Fight for Shelton Bar*.

In 1972 the British Steel Corporation declared its intention to close down inland steel mills, including the newly renovated works in Stoke-on-Trent. Two thousand jobs would have been lost, threatening the economic well-being of the entire district. The Victoria Theatre, by creating *Fight for Shelton Bar*, joined with the local populace in fighting this decision. The documentary provided a colorful and accurate picture of the steelmaking process, as well as coverage of the political decisions being made at both local and national levels. Nightly updated with reports documenting the latest developments in the negotiations, the play became a rallying point for the community. In true agitprop style—and in apparent conflict with Cheeseman's disavowal of political intent—the acting troupe traveled to London, garnered coverage in the national papers, and appeared on the BBC's channel 2. Unquestionably, the documentary drama played a significant part in the efforts of the local steelworks to win a hearing and ultimately to win its case. The theater and the community had become one.

Here is the true purpose of Cheeseman's rendering of the documentary theater enterprise—to sharpen a community's awareness of itself and its roots and, by merging with it, to draw out its potential and influence its future. Following Cheeseman's example, theaters in Hull, Coventry, Liverpool, Bristol, and Nottingham created indigenous documentaries on such diverse subjects as the history of local football teams, the building of sewer systems, and the automobile industry. These plays and their like have not revolutionized the theater. But they have played and continue to play a key role in foregrounding what Sartre articulated as theater's "great fundamental theme, which is, after all, man as event and man as History within the event."[18]

In contrast with this British tradition, documentary dramas in the United States have tended not to be local or regional in character and at the same time more vigorously partisan in political orientation. The major Living Newspapers of the Federal Theater Project were generally national in scope and in their intended audience, even when dealing with a regional phenomenon like the Tennessee Valley Authority. While regional playwriting was encouraged by Hallie Flanagan, she was uncomfortable with plays that were too specifically localized.[19] America has produced much regional drama—from the Texas Trilogy to "historical" pageants involving fictionalized incident and dialogue and commercially produced outdoors for a largely tourist audience. But documentary dramas in the more restricted sense employed here have tended to be event-specific rather than site-specific. Nevertheless, the American branch of the species displays some interesting variations.

Perhaps most typical are trial-transcript plays designed to focus attention on presumed miscarriages of justice. Daniel Berrigan's *The Trial of the Catonsville Nine* (1971) and Eric Bentley's *Are You Now or Have You Ever Been* (1972) are straightforward examples. Emily Mann's *Execution of Justice* (1984) imaginatively juxtaposed elements of the trial of Daniel White, convicted of manslaughter in the death of gay rights activist Harvey Milk, with oral histories and theatrical devices borrowed from the Living Newspaper.

Of special interest are three documentaries that do not fit this mold. Luis Valdez's *Zoot Suit* began as an experimental production of the Mark Taper Forum's "Theater for Now" series and—demonstrating extraordinary local appeal—was soon moved to the mainstage in 1978, and subsequently to Broadway for a short run (58 performances) in 1979. Based on the 1942 murder trial of Henry Reyna, it failed on Broadway precisely because it sacrificed its regional idiosyncrasies (barrio setting, Chicano slang, Teatro Campesino origins) to a hollow theatricality.[20]

Also in 1978, Stephen Schwartz and Nina Faso adapted Studs Terkel's *Working* into a musical, interspersing monologues with songs contributed by James Taylor and others. In the same vein is *Quilters*, developed by the Denver Center Theater Company. Probably the most successful documentary in the history of the American theater, *Quilters* was crafted by Molly Newman and Barbara Damashek out of *The Quilters: Women and Domestic Art* by Patricia Cooper Baker and Norma Buferd—among other nonfiction works. The musical play has been almost constantly in production at regional theaters around the country since the mid-1980s. (It played briefly and not so successfully in New York in 1984.) Relying on the words of otherwise uncelebrated women and employing traditional music for emotional emphasis, *Quilters* eschews the shrill political tone of most American documentaries.

A rich documentary theater tradition has also developed in Canada. Its significant figures include John Grierson himself, who established the National Film Board of Canada; John Coulter, who wrote Canadian Living Newspapers; George Luscombe, who acted with Littlewood's Theater Workshop and founded Toronto Workshop Productions; and Paul Thompson, who worked with Roger Planchon in France and upon returning to Canada created *The Farm Show* with Theatre Passe Muraille. Peter Cheeseman also influenced the development of Canadian documentaries, visiting Toronto in 1972 and providing internships for Canadian directors at the Victoria Theatre in Stoke-on-Trent.

Partly due to Cheeseman's influence, but also because of Canada's geopolitics, Canadian documentary theater has been more local and regional than political. *The Farm*

Show (1972), actor-created from oral histories and performed in an unused barn in Clinton, Ontario, follows the Cheeseman model, as does *Paper Wheat* (1977), which examines the history of the grain industry in Saskatchewan. By contrast, *Buchans—A Mining Town* (1974) is an agit-prop piece specifically designed to influence labor relations in rural Newfoundland. *It's About Time* (1982) is a partly improvised, interactive documentary developed with and for prison inmates in Alberta.[21]

Documentary Theater and the Historian's Art

We have been laboring thus far to set *Steel/City* against a theatrical background on the manifest assumption that it is fundamentally an example of a particular kind of theater. But one could also identify the play as a peculiar example of historical discourse. Put another way: is documentary theater basically fictive images pretending to be facts, or is it facts dressed up in fictive images? Further, is the historical reality the docudrama seeks to convey inexorably devoured by the imaginary component in the art of the theater (as Sartre contends)[22] or is the documentary theater merely a more open-handed example of the fiction-making entailed in factual representation which, according to theorist Hayden White, no historian can escape?[23]

White's controversial contention that poetic and historical narratives draw alike on the same fund of structures and conventions both focuses and complexifies the issues surrounding documentary theater. Unquestionably, history is a narrative, tells a story. How is the historian's narrative different from that of, say, the dramatist? According to White, once one acknowledges that historical events differ from fictive events in that the former have or had space-time locations while the latter are hypothetical—a distinction further obscured by documentary theater—similarities in the narrative enterprise are overwhelming.

Thus, after distinguishing truth of correspondence (i.e., correspondence to "the real") as an objective of history from truth of coherence (that is, logical relatedness) as an objective of fiction, White demonstrates how both forms of discourse aspire to a judicious mixture of both sorts of truth. Crucially, he asserts that the integrity and coherence brought to historical discourse are genuinely and exclusively discursive—that is, fashioned by the historian in the course of his representation of the facts.

White's theory conflates the process by which (a) a conventional playwright selects from among any conceivable and hypothetical sources; (b) a documentary playwright selects from "real" events, characters and dialogue; and (c) a historian structures his selections into historical narrative—for all are obeying the same tropological laws. And it may even be, White suggests, that the structure of language itself dictates the archetypes to which all storytellers are inescapably drawn.

As playwrights producing an example of dramatic discourse, we were reasonably aware of drawing on dramatic conventions. The first act of *Steel/City* resembles a romantic saga or epic; the second suggests a tragedy, though with a distinctly melodramatic cast; and the third act takes the shape of a comedy (it has a "happy" ending) though, in its awareness of unresolved injustices and future uncertainties, an ironic one. White's theory suggests that we were doing more consciously what historians do inadvertently—i.e., casting historical narratives as tragedies, comedies, romances, or ironies.

As historians manqués, however, we were unaware that our narrative strategies and emplotments may have been contaminated with specific—and fluctuating—ideological positions: the first act anarchic (see our scenes of the Whiskey Rebellion and the three Andrew Carnegies); the second radical, in its materialist and mechanistic assumptions; and the third liberal, in its assertion of the persistence of ethnic identity, but with a conservative undercurrent. That

White finds the better historians thus mediating among tropological structures and their ideological demands gives us restrospective—and undeserved—satisfaction.

White's explication of the historical text as a literary artifact implies that the documentary playwright, even when functioning with his cohorts as a historian, can lay no claim to representing "the way things are." Or, more precisely, that the claim to truth of the historian and the claim to truth of the playwright are identical and derived from the fictionalization in which they both engage. But White's argument is not universally accepted. John Clive, for example, is quite aware of the narrative strategy operating in Marx's *Eighteenth Brumaire*. After calling attention to the significance of Marx's initial epigram (after Hegel) that "all facts and personages in world history occur twice, the first time as tragedy, the second time as farce," Clive proceeds to analyze the theatrical imagery of Marx's work in subtle detail. But Clive concludes: "The spellbinding power of the imagery is directly related to the *spell-banishing* power of the historian. Marx's metaphors and similes exert such great effect because they reflect and reinforce his conviction that the realities of class and economic forces underlie a make-believe world of paper slogans and ideological form."[24]

Similarly, John Higham allows that not all invocations of an external reality are suspect. Though it may never yield incontrovertible Truth, the commitment of the historian—or, we might add, the documentary playwright—to explore the boundary between facts and fictions is itself a humanizing effort to be valued, and scrutinized, as an encounter between partisanship and the idealistic impulse to know.[25] This conviction sustained our own paradoxical declaration in the original program notes for *Steel/City* that "Despite its authenticity, *Steel/City* claims neither neutrality nor objectivity. Our point of departure was a determination to follow wherever the facts would lead us; our journey through the city's history left us keen to tell of what we have seen." Whether our leader was Thalia or Clio we leave it to you to decide.

Notes

1. See Peter Weiss, "14 Propositions for a Documentary Theatre," *World Theatre* 18 (1968): 375–89.
2. See *The Documentary Tradition: From Nanook to Woodstock*, ed. Lewis Jacobs (New York: Hopkinson and Blake, 1971), pp. 4–5.
3. David Wright, "Documentary Theater," *Plays and Players* 14 (3 December 1966): 60.
4. "Heinar Kipphardt Pays Tribute to Erwin Piscator," *World Theatre* 17 (1968): 307.
5. See John Willet, *The Theatre of Erwin Piscator* (London: Eyre Methuen, 1978): 186.
6. Arthur Arent, "The Techniques of the Living Newspaper," *Theater Quarterly* 1 (October-December 1971): 57.
7. See *Free, Adult, Uncensored: The Living History of the Federal Theater Project*, ed. John O'Connor and Lorraine Brown (Washington, D.C.: New Republic Books, 1978), p. 14.
8. Charles Marowitz, "Littlewood Pays a Dividend," *Encore* 10 (May–June 1963): 48.
9. Weiss, "14 Propositions for a Documentary Theatre."
10. A. V. Subiotto, "German Documentary Theatre," inaugural lecture delivered at and published by the University of Birmingham, 1972, p. 2.
11. Jack D. Zipes, "Documentary Drama in Germany: mending the circuit," *Germanic Review* 42 (1967): 60.
12. Peter Cheeseman, interview with Gillette Elvgren, Stoke-on-Trent, 12 February 1972.
13. Ibid.
14. Ibid.
15. Ibid.
16. Alfonso Sastre, "Documentary Theatre: Yes and No," *World Theatre* 17 (1968): 393.
17. Cheeseman interview.
18. Jean-Paul Sartre, "Myth and Reality in Theater," in *Sartre on Theater* (New York: Pantheon, 1976), p. 157.
19. George Kazacoff, *Dangerous Theatre: The Federal Theatre Project as a Forum for New Plays* (New York: Peter Lang, 1989), p. 74.
20. See R. G. Davis and Betty Diamond, "Zoot Suit on the Road," *Theatre Quarterly* 9 (Summer 1979): 21–25.
21. See Alan Filewood, *Collective Encounters: Documentary Theatre in English Canada* (Toronto: University of Toronto Press, 1987), on the Canadian tradition.
22. Sartre, "Myth and Reality in Theater," pp. 147–48.
23. For what follows, see especially Hayden White, "The Fictions of Factual Representation" and "The Historical Text as Literary Artifact,"

in *Tropics of Discourse* (Baltimore: Johns Hopkins University Press, 1978).

24. John Clive, "Why Read the Great Nineteenth-Century Historians," *Not by Fact Alone* (Boston: Houghton Mifflin, 1989), p. 36, emphasis added.

25. See especially John Higham, *History. Professional Scholarship in America* (Baltimore: Johns Hopkins University Press, 1989), pp. 265–69.

STEEL/CITY

Steel/City was originally produced by the University of Pittsburgh Theater, March 11–27, 1976. The acting ensemble included:

Rick Aglietti	Jeffrey Kramer
Paul Binotto	David Kuhns
Michael Curran	David Lindberg
Denise Dailey	Mark Lowenthal
Mary Lou Devlin	Don Marshall
Erik Elvgren	Wanda McDaniel
Gillette Elvgren III	Clayton McKinnon
Douglas Farrell	Dennis P. McManus
Francis Favorini	Rob Plotz
Marie Favorini	John Pringle
Bob Federline	D. L. Rinear
Ruth Flaherty	Robin Robinson
Martha Gronsky	Paul Rosa
Lori Grupp	Melanie Smith
Chuck Heckathorne	Rochelle Thompson
Linda Hess	Bill Wendt
Jocelyn Johnson	

Stage Band

Paul Binotto	Paul Rosa
D. L. Rinear	John Yurick

Directed by Gillette Elvgren
Music composed, adapted, and directed by Frank McCarty
Choreography by Margaret Skrinar
Settings and properties by Henry Heymann
Lighting design and technical direction by Richard J. Knowles
Costumes and makeup design by E. H. Pribram

Production Note

The stage setting consists of double-tiered steel scaffolding, which rings the stage and extends down and across the proscenium line toward the audience. A number of large and small kegs and barrels are placed among the scaffolds. The upstage center scaffolding can be slid on and off the stage as needed; otherwise, the basic setting remains onstage for the entire three acts. It is a neutral playing area, transformed by the imagination into the shops or street corners of the first act; the mill, the riverbanks, or the Greasy Spoon boardinghouse of the second act; and so on. Changes in the scenic atmosphere are effected primarily through lighting and projections. A large rear-projection screen hangs about eight feet from the stage floor upstage of the scaffolds and fills the entire width of the stage. Two front-projection screens flank the proscenium arch, and another is situated above the proscenium. This last is used exclusively for title slides (for example "The Carnegie Bandwagon"), while the others carry pictorial images that accompany the action kaleidoscopically throughout. These images are as authentic as the documentary material of the script. Engravings, etchings, watercolor and oil paintings, and other nonphotographic images illuminate the action until the time of the Civil War, when a Matthew Brady photograph of war dead fills the rear screen. Thereafter, photographs predominate.

As the three acts of the play represent three different eras in the life and industry of the city, three different stage images characterize each act. Act 1 is "pioneer Pittsburgh," the rough-and-tumble city of the Whiskey Rebellion and the rugged river boatmen, a city tentative when it came to social graces and which elected a drunken scoundrel and rabble-rouser as one of its mayors. The city forged pig iron in independently owned furnaces manned by Scots-Irish with an all-consuming work ethic. The rhythms and style of the first act reflect this urgent sense of accomplishment and energy. For example, on the neutral stage, the action of a scene begins before the previous scene has been completed. Also, the stage can easily represent more than one place at a time—the locales identified not by cumbersome scenery but through groupings of actors and the ever present projections. In the first act, these consist especially of oil and watercolor paintings, etchings, and woodcuts, with the rivers prominently in evidence and the image of the city smallish, bucolic, but already crowded with belching smokestacks.

Images in the second act are more chiaroscuro. A deliberate effort is made to develop scenes of high contrast, both rhythmically and visually. Tableaux in a melodramatic idiom and imagery from silent film are suggested. Berkman's assassination attempt on Frick is staged in a manner evoking scenes from Griffith's *Intolerance*. The corporate tycoons at the end of the act, in handlebar moustaches and bowlers, might have walked off a Mack Sennett set. Similarly, the music reflects a wide range of moods and styles: solo piano in a honky-tonk vein accompanies Veronica, the "Sweetheart of the South Side"; a gong underscores the dirge for the Homestead strikers; bagpipes or a brass band signal the entrances of Carnegie's forces; organ music comments ironically on the heartless platitudes constituting the "Gospel of Wealth" preached by the rich against the poor.

Act 3 is grounded in the naturalistic imagery of a picnic for retired steelworkers. The projection screens bear an image of the city of Pittsburgh seen at a great distance through leafy trees. The acting style is realistic, a definite change from the presentationalism of the first two acts. In the course of the act, food is cooked onstage, and the smells of sauerkraut and kolbassi waft over the audience. Most of the projected images focus on faces, showing the ethnic variety of the city's people, and the whole act has the feel of a family get-together: stories and jokes are told; pictures passed around; there is card playing, drinking. Within this framework, the flashbacks are more nostalgic, aiming to capture the feel of how people remember rather than attempting to determine the accuracy of their recollections—except for the 1919 strike episode, which is meant to have the impact of a Living Newspaper. The final note is elegaic and, relative to the demise of the steel industry, somewhat prophetic.

Musical Note

Most of the music for the drama originates from the specific period or incident celebrated in song. Thus, "Way Down the Ohio" dates from about 1810, "The Homestead Strike" is an authentic strike song from 1892. We have, however, allowed ourselves a liberty we have not taken with the dialogue: we've altered or augmented the lyrics of songs in order to strengthen a narrative line or to make reference to local figures.

Both live and taped music are employed. The live music is sung by the cast, normally accompanied in acts 1 and 2 by the stage band—consisting of guitar, double bass, banjo, violin, and/or mandolin. (Exceptions: "Soho on Saturday Night" is accompanied by solo piano; "The Homestead Strike" by two guitars only.) In the third act, the band plays East European equivalents of the American instruments. On tape: Lafayette's quadrille (chamber ensemble), Carnegie's band music (brass band), accompaniment to "America the Beautiful" (orchestra), a dirge (double bass and gong), and various bagpipe effects.

Note on Casting

Steel/City has hundreds of roles which can be played comfortably with a cast of thirty, including actor/musicians.

Doubling assignments should be made for thematic impact (for example, the same actor can play Berkman and Schwab), as well as for logistical convenience.

Act 1

Scene 1 / Early Pittsburgh

(Title slide: April 22, 1794)

Dim up an idyllic slide of the sparsely populated city in the 1790s. Lights up on the STAGE BAND, *which plays a Scots-Irish tune. The people of the town drift in, perhaps doing a simple dance to the music. They take their places around the scaffolds and strike a tableau. Enter the* TOWN CRIER, *ringing a bell. The tableau breaks.*

CRIER: Whereas the inhabitants of the town of Pittsburgh, in the county of Allegheny, have by their petition, prayed to be incorporated, and that the said town and its vicinity as hereafter described should be erected into a borough; and whereas it may contribute to the advantage of the inhabitants of said town and also to those who trade and resort there; and to the public utility, that nuisances, encroachments of all sorts; contentions, annoyances . . . *(He lowers his voice, realizing that he is the biggest annoyance in the town.)*
and inconveniences in the said town and its vicinity should be prevented. Be it enacted that the said town of Pittsburgh is hereby erected into a borough, which shall be called the Borough of Pittsburgh, forever.

(The town comes to life. The business of small trade is carried on. Enter HUGH HENRY BRACKENRIDGE, *an elegant figure, who speaks with a slight Scots burr.)*

BRACKENRIDGE: Pittsburgh. It appeared to me as what would one day be a town of note. *(Sound of printing press in background.* BRACKENRIDGE *strolls to "Gazette" office, where editors are hanging freshly printed newspapers out to dry.)* I have heard it said that you are about to publish a *Gazette* in the town of Pittsburgh. A principal advan-

tage will be to know what is going on in our own state, particularly what our representatives are doing in Philadelphia.
(CITIZENS *and* TRADESPEOPLE *enter, carrying props indicating their professions.*)

CITIZEN #1: One skin dresser and breeches maker; one stocking weaver . . .

BRACKENRIDGE: The town consists at present of about a hundred dwelling houses with building appurtenant. More are daily added.

EDITOR: *(Correcting him.)* Thirty-six log houses, one stone house, one frame house, five *small* stores.

TRADESMAN #1: Scythes and sickles to be had on the shortest notice for either cash, ginseng, or country produce at William Dunning.
(*Hangs placard on shop. Other* TRADESPEOPLE *follow suit. In act 1, scene 3, the verso sides of these placards, on which the names of iron craft firms are lettered, will be turned to face the audience.*)

TRADESMAN #2: At George McGunnigle, Market Street: locks, keys, hinges, grates, shovels, tongs, pokers, flesh forks, pipe tomahawks, currycombs, scalping knives.

BRACKENRIDGE: There is not a more delightful spot under the heaven to spend any of the summer months than at this place. . . .

CITIZEN #2: One brewer and malster . . .

CITIZEN #3: A large and general assortment of European and West Indian goods available at Eliot, Williams, and Company.

BRACKENRIDGE: Nor is the winter season enjoyed with less festivity than in more populous and cultivated towns.

CITIZEN: Umbrellas, women's beaver hats, playing cards,

writing paper and quills, Jamaica spirits, West Indian rum, corkscrews . . .
(Sound of popping cork; INNKEEPER *or* MAID *hangs out placard that reads: Whale and Monkey Inn.)*

INNKEEPER:
Here the weary may rest
The hungry feed
And those who thirst
May quaff the best.
(A bedraggled WAITRESS *spits into a beer mug, polishes it with a dirty rag, and hands it to a scowling visitor. He carries a carpet bag.)*

DR. SCHOEPF: *(At the inn.)* Pittsburgh is inhabited almost entirely by Scots and Irish who live in paltry loghouses, and are as dirty as in the north of Ireland or even Scotland.
(Leaving the inn.)
There is a great deal of small trade carried on. . . .

CITIZEN: One ropemaker; five blacksmiths.

DR. SCHOEPF: *(To* BRACKENRIDGE.*)* There are in the town four attorneys, two doctors, and not a priest of any persuasion, nor church, nor chapel; so that they are likely to be damned without benefit of clergy. The place, I believe, will never be very considerable.

BRACKENRIDGE: *(Disagreeing.)* This town in future will be the place of great manufactury. Such is our distance from either of the oceans that the importation of heavy articles will be expensive. The manufacture of them will therefore become more an object here than elsewhere.

CITIZEN: Thomas Wylie, corner of Third and Market; all kinds of mill irons turned in the neatest manner.
(As BRACKENRIDGE *delivers the following speech with great civic pride, inspired by the vision he conjures up, a rough-hewn farmer,* BRADFORD, *enters and gestures for*

the attention of the TOWNSPEOPLE, *who group around him.)*

BRACKENRIDGE: Who knows what families of fortune may emigrate to this place? In the fall of the year and during the winter season there is usually a great concourse of strangers at this place, about to descend to the westward. It must appear like enchantment to a stranger . . . to see all at once and on the verge of the inhabited globe, a town with smoking chimneys, halls lighted up with splendor, ladies and gentlemen assembled, various music and the mazes of the dance. He may suppose it to be the effect of magic, or that he is come to a new world where there is all the refinement of the former, and more benevolence of heart.
(A rowdy crowd led by BRADFORD *advances on* BRACKENRIDGE, *who retreats to the "Gazette" office, where an* EDITOR *is taking cover.)*

BRADFORD: *(To* BRACKENRIDGE, *brandishing a whiskey jug.)* I presume you have heard of the spirited opposition given to the excise laws of this state. The crisis is now come. We have determined with head, heart, hand, and voice that we will support the opposition to the excise law. By all the ties that a *union* of interests can suggest, we solicit you to join with us.
(The CROWD *seconds him.)*

BRACKENRIDGE: *(Incredulous; to audience.)* A town meeting was assembled about dusk; almost the whole of the town convened. The prevailing idea was to burn the town of Pittsburgh!

Scene 2 / The Whiskey Rebellion, 1794

(Title slide: Whiskey Rebellion, 1794)

The angry CROWD *takes the stage and sings and dances the following:*

CROWD: *(Singing.)*
    Oh Whiskey you're the divil,
    You're leading me astray.
    (Chorus:) Oh, Whiskey you're the divil drunk or sober!

    It's the only thing we make here
    That brings us any pay. (Chorus)

    Now they say that Mr. Hamilton
    Will take our stills away. (Chorus)

    The excise man from Philly
    Was crafty, mean, and sly. (Chorus)

    He came to tax our whiskey,
    Our Monongahela Rye. (Chorus)

    It fell within the month of June
    In the year of ninety-four. (Chorus)

    The country folk uprising broke
    Into a wild uproar. (Chorus)
    (They dance a wild country reel.)

    At Braddock's Field the farmers met
    To march upon the town. (Chorus)

    But fifteen barrels of whiskey
    Lay most upon the ground. (Chorus)

    And then behold an army came
    The excise to maintain. (Chorus)

    They camped before the farmers' door
    Full fifteen thousand men. (Chorus)

The rebels took to running,
The army they did flee. (Chorus)

Come morning in the valley,
They'll all be drinking tea. (Chorus)

The little man got nothing
On that you must agree. (Chorus)

So, come morning in the valley,
We'll all be drinking tea. (Chorus)
(The CROWD *disperses.* BRACKENRIDGE *and the* EDITOR *creep gingerly out from under cover, as the rebels leave the stage.)*

BRACKENRIDGE: *(Warning the* EDITOR.*)* If you print an almanac, I would advise you to leave out all profane songs, *(Removes his hat respectfully.)*
except in the praise of General Washington.

(BLACKOUT)

Scene 3 / Iron City

(Title slide: Pittsburgh Becomes the Iron City, 1800–1825)

In the blackout the sound of a squeaking wheelbarrow is heard; also the clink of metal implements. The lights dim up on a relaxed crowd of WORKERS *about to begin their day. In contrast to the previous town scene, they are not* TRADESPEOPLE *but* WORKERS, *most of whom are involved in the iron industry. Likewise in contrast to "Early Pittsburgh," the feeling of the scene as it progresses is not that of a friendly group setting up shop, but of a determined, vigorous band of workers earning their bread. The activity of the scene has the rhythm of a workday, with a lunch break and a peak of activity in midafternoon. The various noises of ironmaking are created by the actors and their props and tools, not by taped machine noises. It should be clear to the audience that the* WORKERS *are in charge of their work and their machines, not the machines of them. At the sound of a whistle, the* WORKERS *shake off the last vestiges of sleep and start their work. As the scene progresses, projections convey the changing profile of Pittsburgh's skyline. By the end of the scene, mills with pleasantly billowing smokestacks predominate. Emerging from the* CROWD *is the engaging, bespectacled figure of the almanacker,* ZADOK CRAMER. *He could be played by the actor who previously took the part of the* EDITOR.*)*

CRAMER: *(Expansively, gesturing to* CROWD *starting its work.)* The whole town may be likened unto a large workshop, in which are a great variety of businesses briskly carried on by hundreds of ingenious and active workmen, determined to live by their honest labors.

WORKER: Here are the materials for every species of manufacture, and these means have been taken advantage of by skillful and industrious artisans and mechanics from all parts of the world.

WORKER: A mixture of all nations: Irish, Scotch, English, French, Dutch, Swiss.

WORKER: *(Indicating* ANTHONY BEELEN.*)* The manufacture of iron in all the different branches, and the mills of all sorts.

BEELEN: Anthony Beelen begs to inform his friends and the public that he has established an air foundry on the banks of the Monongahela, which is now ready to execute orders for brewers, soap boilers, salt kettles, and generally every kind of castings.

(Title slide: $56,598 in Iron Products—1803)

CITIZEN: I can remember the erection of Cowan's Rolling Mill, and the important day on which the engine was put into operation. A large number of citizens had gathered to witness that event.
*(*CITIZENS *assemble in a crowd and reenact the scene as it is described, struggling vigorously to force the flywheel to begin moving.)*
When the time came and the engineer let on the steam, there was much whistling and blowing, but no answering motion came from the great stubborn flywheel. A call for help was made, and the bystanders armed themselves with levers and handspikes and went at the wheel. It went off as a thing of life, and the engine of Pittsburgh's first rolling mill was sturdily at work.

MECHANIC: *(Deprecating the evidently much smaller steam engine at Cowan's, this fellow is excited tremendously by technology.)*
A steam engine of seventy horsepower moves the slitting and rolling mill together with the nail factory of Stackpoole and Whiting. So powerful is the mechanism employed that I have seen more than three hundred nails made in a minute with the aid of one man.

GENERAL O'HARA: *(Proudly holding aloft a glass bottle.)* Today we made the first bottle at a cost of thirty thousand dollars!
(His hand is struck by a clumsy WORKER. *Bottle falls and smashes.)*

VISITOR: *(A lady of the streets, trying to win the attention of the busy* WORKERS.*)* Nowhere in the world is everyone so regularly and continually busy as in Pittsburgh. I do not believe there is on the face of the earth, including the U.S., a single town in which the idea of amusement so seldom enters the heads of the inhabitants. Pittsburgh is therefore one of the least amusing cities in the world; there is no interruption of business for six days in the week, except during the three meals.
(Whistle blows for lunch. Everyone relaxes. One takes out a guitar or banjo.)

WHISKEY SALESMAN: *(Played by one of the* WHISKEY REVELERS, *he delivers his spiel like a flim-flam man.)* There are four distilleries in the city. Among these we must not forget the establishment of Mr. George Sutton, who is the manufacturer of the celebrated Tuscaloosa, which has been drunk from Maine to Georgia and which is so highly esteemed for its antimiasmatic qualities; for the mildness with which it insurges the consumer; and for the fresh and exhilarated spirits that it gives to those who may have been accidentally rendered obsolete by its power. It steals upon the senses like music upon the soul,
(The opening six notes of the "Whiskey" number are played on the banjo or guitar.)
and animates the intellect without ever collapsing an idea.

BRITISH VISITOR: *(Walking contemptuously among relaxed* WORKERS.*)* By what strange infatuation they could have been attracted towards this city—no tall brick buildings, no towering steeples, no elegant commodious edifices . . .

not a single public square save the dirty contracted spot of ground, the Diamond—the hopes of finding banknotes among the heaps of dust and clouds of smoke?

MECHANIC: *(Proudly, and explaining the scientific background.)* The smoke of bituminous coal is antimiasmatic. It is sulphurous and antiseptic, and hence it is, perhaps, that no putrid disease has ever been known to spread in the place. Strangers with weak lungs for a while find their coughs aggravated by the smoke; but nevertheless, asthmatic patients have found relief in breathing it. In comparison with the western cities, including Cincinnati, *(The* CROWD *groans.)* there is less bilious fever, less ague and fever, and less cholera infantum.
*(*BRITISH VISITOR *is driven off. A whistle blows, and all return to work.)*

CRAMER: For patriotic industry, Pittsburgh is not exceeded by any place of its kind in the world.

(Title slide: $94,890 in Iron Products—1810)

Our rising manufactures are the surest and most solid basis on which the country can rest its future independence and happiness. Let the maddened nations of Europe rinse their hands in each other's blood. Americans, be at peace, be honest, be industrious!
(The ensemble hits a steady work rhythm, interrupted by a CITIZEN *who rushes in.)*

CITIZEN: Citizens, I embrace the first opportunity to inform you that war has been declared!
(Slide of declaration of war from Pittsburgh "Gazette.")
This measure passed in the House of Representatives by a majority of thirty and in the Senate nineteen to thirteen. This is an unqualified, unconditional war, by land

Act 1: Scene 3 / 19

and sea, against the United Kingdom of Great Britain and Ireland!
(Enthusiastic whoops and hollers, as the ensemble goes back to work with doubled effort.)

(Title slide: $764,200 in Iron Products—1815)

(Work rhythms build to a fever pitch. Whistle blows, ending the workday. Great, weary sigh from WORKERS. *As the stage slowly begins to clear, a* VISITOR *enters.)*

VISITOR: I entered the smoky Pittsburgh, more than ever charmed with the scenery amidst which it is seated—still beautiful despite the ravages of the mines and the pollution of all the useful abominations attendant upon the manufacture of iron. The wealth and various attractions of this rich heiress of nature have proved her undoing.
(Lights dim slowly.)

WORKER: But to see them go home loaded with turkey, fowl, fat beef, fresh butter, clearly evinces that they not only live, but live well.
(He leaves.)

CITIZEN: *(Watching the last* WORKER *leave—with nostalgia.)* Yet, what have we gained by trade, and all other desirable things, compared with the artless manners and delightful amusements, which we have lost? Chartered as we are, as a city corporation, do we enjoy the real, unfashionable contentment with which our village predecessors were blessed? Where are our pleasant, social tea-drinkings, our sturdy, blindman's bluff, our evening chitchat, in which both sexes participated, without a thought of visiting cards? Where are the strawberry huntings, the charming promenades . . . ?

(FADE OUT)

Scene 4 / The Riverboat Era

In the dark, the STAGE BAND *plays the opening bars of "Way Down the Ohio." Dim up on rear screen, a river scene with Pittsburgh's billowing smokestacks in the distance.* BOATMEN *enter as lights come up.*

CAPTAIN: Stand to your poles!

BOATMAN #1: Shippin' in: Onondaga salt.

BOATMAN #2: Shippin' out: iron.

BOATMAN #3: Cast Iron.

BOATMAN #1: Wrought iron.

BOATMAN #2: Wire.

BOATMAN #3: Nails.

BOATMAN #1: Hoops.

BOATMAN #2: Tools.

CAPTAIN: We call at:

BOATMAN #1: Wheeling.

BOATMAN #2: Big Bone Lick.

BOATMAN #3: *(Disgustedly.)* Cincinnati.

BOATMAN #1: Shawneetown.

BOATMAN #2: Devil's Elbow.

BOATMAN #3: Hull's Left Leg.

CAPTAIN: Destination New Orleans!
   (The BAND *sings, and* BOATMEN *dance a strenuous dance with the long poles used by keelboatmen.)*

Act 1: Scene 4 / 21

BAND: *(Singing.)*

> Way down the Ohio, this old barge I steer
> In hopes that some pretty gal, on the bank, will appear.
> I'll hug her and kiss her, till I've had my fill,
> Then I'll go find another girl down by the mill.
>
> The river is rough, and it runs wide and long.
> The current flows in my blood, it is where I belong.
> I love you, Ohio, you're more than a wife,
> You're the constant companion through all of my life.
>
> The poling is hard, but my back it is strong.
> I sing to the rhythm of the Ohio's sweet song.
> When I've poled up river, I throw out my chest,
> For I know I'm the man who can do it the best.
>
> Way down the Ohio, I know where I'm bound.
> I steer towards the muddy banks, back in old Pittsburgh town.
> A cargo of trade goods, I bring from the west,
> To exchange for the iron that Pittsburgh makes best.
> *(At the end, a loud steamboat whistle blows.)*

TECHNOCRAT: *(Played by same actor who expressed enthusiasm for technology in previous scene, or by an Establishment figure.)* With pleasure we announce that the Steam Boat lately built at Pittsburgh, the *Orleans* by Nicholas Roosevelt, fully answers the most sanguine expectations that were formed of her sailing.
(Grumbles and snorts from the BOATMEN.*)*
A novel sight to see a huge boat working her way up the windings of the Ohio, without the appearance of sail, or pole, or any manual labor about her—moving with the secrets of her own wonderful mechanism, and propelled by power undiscoverable.

CAPTAIN: It's a scheme to destroy our business and expose people's lives!

BOATMAN #1: *(Mocking.)* Like to see that newfangled machine try Horsetail Ripple or Letart's Falls!

BOATMAN #2: To get up them without the aid of good settin' poles.

BOATMAN #3: It could not be done, no how!
(Laughter, as BOATMEN *leave.)*

Scene 5 / Lafayette

(Title slide: Pittsburgh's High Society, 1825)

The hearty laughter of BOATMEN *is echoed by the more delicate and effete laughter of Pittsburgh's high society: a* CROWD *that enters silhouetted at the rear of the stage. They carry banners and escort* GENERAL LAFAYETTE *with great élan downstage.*

LAFAYETTE'S ESCORT: Here the British troops under Braddock were defeated by the French and Indians in 1755.

RICH CITIZEN: *(As sights are being pointed out to the general.)* The general was struck with the excellence and perfection of the processes employed in the various workshops which he examined.

LAFAYETTE: *(Speaking with a French accent.)* The patriotic gratification I feel at the sight of your beautiful manufacture is enhanced by the friendly reception I have met from you.
(CITIZENS *murmur appreciatively. Lights brighten. Elegant music. The ripple of conversation.)*

SOCIETY LADY: *(Gushing.)* It's Lafayette fever!
(An elegant quadrille is danced, as LAFAYETTE *watches courteously. A single paisley shawl is passed from woman to woman during the dance. On the screens, fashion plates of the era are projected.)*

LAFAYETTE'S ESCORT: *(Introducing each couple to the* GENERAL.*)* Mr. and Mrs. Thomas Barlow.
(She flashes the extravagant paisley shawl, which is passed surreptitiously from woman to woman as each is introduced to LAFAYETTE. *Faint music in the background.)*

LAFAYETTE: How do you do?

ESCORT: The Honorable Judge Charles Shaler and Mrs. Shaler.

LAFAYETTE: How do you do?

ESCORT: Mayor John M. Snowden.

LAFAYETTE: How do you do?

ESCORT: Mr. and Mrs. Henry Baldwin. Iron manufacture.

LAFAYETTE: How do you do?
(The dance ends. A BUTLER *serves glasses for a toast.)*

SHALER: *(Getting the* GENERAL's *attention.)* General Lafayette. When you left us, the spirit of commerce had scarce awakened in our seaports; now, there is no harbor so remote that is not whitened with our canvas; no nation that does not respect our flag. Receive then, this nation's homage, in the name of those who will survive the day in which your right to it was acquired.

LAFAYETTE: To the City of Pittsburgh.
(Appreciative murmurs from CITIZENS.*)*
May its manufacturing prosperity more and more increase under the auspices of republican freedom, the most powerful engine in the universe.
(Everyone drinks. Music grows louder. As CITIZENS *leave,* LAFAYETTE *steps forward and addresses the audience in mock wonder.)*
I have never before seen so many paisley shawls as those worn by the women in Pittsburgh.

(MUSIC AND LIGHTS FADE OUT)

Scene 6 / Pittsburgh, 1850

(Title Slide: Pittsburgh, 1850)

Two elegant onlookers from previous scene come forward. One wears a hooded white satin cape. She is spotlighted and admires herself demurely in an imaginary mirror, as her companion speaks.

REPORTER: One of the most exquisitely beautiful women in Pittsburgh in early times was Miss Eliza Tiernan. An ivorylike complexion without a particle of color, perfection of form and features. About this time the Sisters of Mercy located in the city.
(Lights up on two SISTERS, *in capes like* ELIZA's—*only black; they come forward and position themselves on either side of* ELIZA.*)*
Which order Miss Tiernan ultimately joined, and a sight never to be forgotten was that on the day on which, in a magnificent bridal robe, she stood before the bishop in all her bewildering maidenly beauty and formally renounced the world, its pleasures, and vanities.
(The SISTERS *cover her head with the hood and lead her off.)*
This peerless woman died in a very few years of ship fever contracted by service in the hospital.
(He leaves. Cross fade to steerage of an immigrant ship, a huddle of very sick people, gasping and moaning. The SISTERS *move among them.)*

FRANCES WARDE: *(Tending one of the sick.)* We are Irish Sisters of Mercy, sent for by Bishop Michael O'Connor to staff the new Diocese of Pittsburgh.

ANOTHER SISTER: We visit the steerage daily as well as the second cabin. Accommodations in both are poor enough.

ANOTHER SISTER: *(Walking among immigrants.)* On the

eighth of May, 1847, the *Urania* from Cork, with several hundred immigrants on board, a large proportion of them sick and dying of ship fever, was put into quarantine. This was the first of the plague-smitten ships from Ireland. One half of the entire number are in different stages of the disease; many dying, some dead, the fatal poison intensified by the indescribable foulness of the air breathed and rebreathed by the gasping sufferers.

FRANCES WARDE: Many of the people were helped by our work of mercy—some said that if anything should bring them to Pittsburgh, they would pay a visit to the sisters.

ANOTHER SISTER: We never saw any of them again.

(BLACKOUT)

In the dark, crude male laughter is heard, as if a smutty joke had just been told. Dim up on rear screen a projection of a street-corner crowd, Pittsburgh 1850. Lights up on JOSEPH BARKER *haranguing a crowd of men, in tableau. He wears a stovepipe hat, white necktie, and large cape. Women on the fringes of the crowd leave, insulted, as he speaks. One of the women crosses the stage and engages in conversation with a bystander and policeman, who eye* BARKER *carefully.*

BARKER: Great God! When we see the mighty death-days of that beautiful and once famed Ireland; when we see how the dusky, glaring torch of popery has shaken its serpent hair into terror of terrors, and danced to its neck in Protestant blood, should we not strive and pray that papal Ireland may not now be a tar-barrel, to light our highways to ruin and death!
(Turning to his associate.)
That's true, isn't it, Kirtland?

KIRTLAND: Every word of it, and I have the papers here to prove it!

(Loud laughter.)

MCLEAN: *(Bystander to* POLICEMAN, *with Irish accent.)* I live in the Fifth Ward near the canal, and keep a grocery; saw the meetings as I was going to church; saw them in Penn Street, there were large crowds on both sides of the street.

DR. HAZLETT: *(Also talking to* POLICEMAN.*)* I heard them read from Roman Catholic books and I thought they were very obscene. Why, Joseph Barker quoted *Den's Theology*. When he was talking about marriage, he said . . .

BARKER: The young man had to go once to the priest, but the young woman had to go three times, and the priest informed her, after saying a Latin nostrum or two to her, that he had to consecrate her womb, and then he lifted up her clothes and . . .
(Suggestive gesture.)
at her. That's true, isn't it, Kirtland?

KIRTLAND: Every word of it, and I have the papers here to prove it!

JAMES MURPHY: He called the church a . . .

BARKER: Whorehouse.

MURPHY: He said that the Catholic women were many of them . . .

BARKER: Prostitutes.

MURPHY: He used language that no man should use. He said that the . . .

BARKER: Pope and clergy are holy water sons of bitches. . . .
*(*POLICEMAN *arrests* BARKER, *drags him off.* CROWD *laughs, begins to chant "Barker for Mayor." An earnest* CROWD *enters with placards, shouting "Guthrie for Mayor!" and "Elect McCutcheon!" There is a brief parade and shouting match among various political supporters.)*

28 / STEEL/CITY

A WOMAN: *(Rushing in with a newspaper.)* Joseph Barker elected mayor!
(The CROWD *indicates disbelief and gathers around.)*

(Title slide: A Bigot in City Hall)

MAN: It is a fixed fact that Joseph Barker has been elected mayor of the City of Pittsburgh.

WOMAN: Barker leaves jail to go almost triumphantly into the mayoralty.

ANOTHER WOMAN: Governor William F. Johnston pardons Barker.
(BARKER *is carried in on the shoulders of his supporters, all men. A hush falls on the* CROWD, *which can barely contain its laughter during the following.)*

JUDGE PATTON: *(To* BARKER.*)* I hope, sir, you may more than realize the expectations of your friends by an honest, impartial, and energetic discharge of your duties.

BARKER: Gentlemen of the Select and Common Councils, in the position in which I stand in relation to you, . . . I have not the strength. . . . Read this. . . .
(Hands papers to KIRTLAND.*)*

KIRTLAND: I thank all of you for the honor conferred upon me. I urge new and more stringent laws against doggeries and hustering. I declare I will punish only lawbreakers.

BARKER: That's true, isn't it, Kirtland?

KIRTLAND: Every word of it, and I have the papers here to prove it!
(The rowdy CROWD *exits, as another* CROWD *enters bearing picket signs: "$6.00 for Boilers," "$4.00 for Puddling," "No Reduction of Wages." Chants of "Down with the Iron-*

masters!" An organizer, MATTHEWS, *silences the* CROWD. *During the following speeches, projections of mills with heavily billowing smoke fill the screens. Also, scenes of* PUDDLERS' *work.)*

MATTHEWS: *(Atop one of the scaffolds.)* We, the puddlers, do the labor; others are drones—we produce wealth; others accumulate. This strike for a reduction of our wages is an effort to grind us down to the dust!
(CROWD *shouts agreement. Action freezes in a tableau.)*

PUDDLER: *(Appearing in a spotlight across from* MATTHEWS, *with a puddler's rabble in his hands.)* An iron puddler boils the impurities out of pig iron and changes it into that finer product, wrought iron. The working door of the puddling furnace is a porthole opening on a sea of flame. My palms and fingers, scorched by the heat, are hardened like goat hooves.
(The CROWD *breaks out of its freeze.)*

MATTHEWS: Our employers say they cannot help us; they say they are making nothing. But all the while they live in luxury, in pomp, and in ease. The proprietors tell us that they are not making anything because they have no market for their iron; and that the remedy is a reduction in our wages. Now I would like to ask them how a reduction in wages will augment the demand or in any way improve the market?
(CROWD *freezes as before.)*

PUDDLER: If you want to know what it is like to be a puddler, strap a twenty-five-pound weight to your arm and do calisthenics ten hours in a room so hot it melts your eyebrows.
(Light out on PUDDLER.*)*

MATTHEWS: (CROWD *breaks its freeze.)* Our employers will never abandon their effort to put us under. Therefore, we had better prepare for them while we have the power. We must organize!

(CROWD *reacts with some uncertainty.*)
We have an example before us in the Iron Moulders of Cincinnati.
(*Some grumbles from the* CROWD, *who are tired of hearing about Cincinnati.*)
They have organized. They divide wages and profits among themselves. Why should we not have the enormous profits of this business as well as those who work not? Let us stand together. We can live as long as they can. We shall not starve in this land of plenty!

SMISK: *(One of the* CROWD.*)* My name is Smisk. I'm a puddler from the East. Let me state that from fifteen to twenty agents have been employed in the east by the Pittsburgh Iron Masters to induce workmen to come to this city, and that they received five dollars per head for the men so procured.
(*Downstage, an* IRONMASTER *enters, accompanied by a few* SCABS.)

IRONMASTER: The Eastern puddlers work more economically, and are generally more intelligent. The introduction of these new workmen will break up the old monopoly and will give a chance to all, on equal terms, to compete for these valuable situations. (*He hands them money and urges them to enter his mill. The* CROWD *grumbles, and begins to shout "Scab!" "Strikebreakers!" "Go back to Philadelphia!" Labor is our capital!" "Taking an honest man's job!" "Close up the mill!" "March on Graff's Rolling Mill!" The* CROWD *urges its* WOMEN *forward. Most of the* SCABS *flee the angry mob.*)

CROWD: "It's us who's been suppressed!" "Dirty Scab!" "Stone the furnace!" "Ay, choke it with coal!" "Shut down Graff's Rolling Mill!" "And Shoenberger's!" "And Bailey's!" "Stop the Mill!"
(*They grab one of the* SCABS *who has not run off. Encouraged by the* MEN, *the* WOMEN *lift him above their heads.* MAYOR BARKER *enters. The* MAYOR *carries a pistol.*)

Act 1: Scene 6 / 31

BARKER: Citizens, ladies . . . I implore you. . . .

CROWD: *(Roars, surges forward.)* "To the river!" "Let's see if scabs can swim!" "Drown him!" "One, two . . . !"
(They are about to throw the SCAB *in the river. A pistol shot rings out as* BARKER *shoots. Silence.)*

A WOMAN RIOTER: Wait! It isn't for murder that we're about.
(The CROWD, *disgruntled, disperses. A short, bearded young man in knickers appears in a pool of light—young* ANDREW CARNEGIE. *He picks up a wallet, which has apparently been lost by one in the* CROWD.)

POLICEMAN: *(Barely visible on the edge of the light.)* A messenger boy of the name of Andrew Carnegie, employed by the O'Reilly Telegraph Company, yesterday found a draft for the amount of five hundred dollars. Like an honest little fellow, he promptly made known the fact, and deposited the paper in good hands where it waits identification.
*(*ANDY *pockets the wallet and starts off furtively. The* POLICEMAN *repeats, admonishingly.)*
Like an honest little fellow, he *promptly* made known the fact, and deposited the paper in good hands where it waits identification.
*(*ANDY *sighs, changes direction, and marches off.)*

(BLACKOUT)

Scene 7 / The Rise of Carnegie

(Title slide: Carnegie Ascendant)

During the blackout, a Scots air is heard, played on bagpipes, recalling the tune that began the act. Enter three ANDREW CARNEGIES—*the young man from the previous scene and two others similarly dressed and bearded—doing a Highland fling. There is always a* CARNEGIE *in the right place at the right time. Most of the time the three* ANDYS *speak and move together—sometimes in unison, occasionally dividing a single sentence among them and speaking it seriatim.*

ANDY #1: *(Innocently.)* My first position, a bobbin boy. First work down there at one dollar and twenty cents per week. It was a hard life. In the winter Father and I had to rise and breakfast in the darkness, reach the factory before it was daylight, and with a short interval for lunch, work till after dark.
(His FATHER, *a gray shape in the background, is seen stirring and holding out a hand to little* ANDY *as they move to the factory.)*
The hours hung heavily upon me and in the work itself I took no pleasure; but the cloud had a silver lining, as it gave me a feeling I was doing something for the world and my family.
(His FATHER *leads him off rather brusquely.)*

ANDY #2: My position as messenger boy soon made me acquainted with the few leading men of the city. The bar of Pittsburgh was distinguished. Judge Wilkins was at its head, and he and Judge McCandless, Judge McClure, Charles Shaler, and his partner Edwin Stanton, afterwards the great War Secretary, were all well known to me. In business circles... Thomas Howe, James Park, John Chalfant, and Benjamin F. Jones were great

men to whom the messenger boys looked as models. Mr. Jones. . . .
(JONES *enters. The two other* ANDYS *appear to block his path, and* ANDY #2 *runs to* JONES *and gives him a telegram.*)

JONES: *(Muttering as he reads.)* James Laughlin. Partnership. The South Side.
(He looks up, envisioning his name on a huge sign.)
The American Iron and Steel Works. Jones and Laughlin!
(He starts to leave, but ANDY #2 *clears his throat, and all three* ANDYS *extend their right hands. At a loss,* JONES *tosses a quarter in the air and exits. A scramble.* ANDY #2 *comes up with it. Others leave.*)

ANDY #2: It was reckoned a great triumph among the boys to deliver a message upon the street. And there was the additional satisfaction to the boy himself, that a great man, stopped upon the street in this fashion, seldom failed to notice the boy and compliment him.

ANDY #3: *(He enters clacking a telegraph key; the other two* ANDYS *follow him.)* I have got past delivering messages now and have got to operating. I am to have . . .
(All three ANDYS *speak together.)*
four dollars a week and good prospects of getting more.

JAMES REID: *(Across the stage.)* I liked the boy's looks, and it was very easy to see that though he was little, he was full of spirit.
(The three ANDYS *are busily at work;* REID *turns, walks toward them, and is confused at finding three.*)
He had not been with me a month when he began to ask whether I would teach him to telegraph. I began to instruct him and found him an apt pupil.

ANDY #3: The result was that I began as a telegraph operator at the tremendous salary of . . .

(All three ANDYS *speak together.)*
twenty-five dollars per month, which I thought was a fortune.
(The sound of a steam locomotive is heard, and a slide is projected. It appears to cross the upstage area. The three ANDYS *watch it go past.)*

ANDY #1: I have some news to tell you. I have left my old place in the telegraph office and am now in the employ of the Pennsylvania Railroad Company. I had now stepped into the open world, and the change at first was far from agreeable. This was a different world, indeed, from that to which I had been accustomed. I ate, necessarily, of the fruit of the tree of knowledge of good and evil for the first time. But there were still the sweet and pure surroundings of home, where nothing coarse or wicked ever entered.

ANDY'S MOTHER *(Entering with a lunch pail.)*
Ye'll try the world soon my lad,
And Andrew dear, believe me,
Ye'll find mankind an unco squad,
And muckle they may grieve ye:
(Sternly.)
For care and trouble set your thought,
Ev'n when your end's attained;
And a' your views may come to nought,
Where every nerve is strained.
*(*ANDY *reacts with a stealthy look around him. She hands out the lunch pail. A scramble, as before over the coin.* ANDY #2 *wins.)*

SCOTT: *(In a spot, and with a handful of bills.)* You know, I think it would be right to start you at fifteen hundred dollars.
(At this, the three ANDYS *rush pell-mell to* SCOTT.*)*
And after a while, if you succeed, you will get the eighteen hundred. Would that be satisfactory?

3 ANDYS: *(Speaking seriatim, dividing the lines among them.)* "Oh, please, . . . Mr. Scott," . . . I said,
(Together.)
"Don't speak to me of money."
(ANDY #2 grabs the bills from SCOTT, who leaves.)

ANDY #3: It was not a case of mere hire and salary, and then and there my promotion was sealed. I was to have a department to myself. Orders between Pittsburgh and Altoona would now be signed A. C. That was glory enough for me.
(The sound of cannon makes the three ANDYS jump. A crowd of WORKERS enter, led by a MAN brandishing a newspaper.)

MAN: War commenced!
(The three ANDYS take off in three different directions.)

WOMAN: The batteries opened at Fort Sumter!

MAN: The war bills passed at Harrisburg!

WOMAN: Appointments by the president!
(She gestures to the three ANDYS as they march on with SCOTT, who hands one a certificate. A scramble. ANDY #3 comes up with it.)

ANDY #3: I was at once summoned to Washington by Mr. Scott, who had been appointed assistant secretary of war in charge of the Transportation Department. I was to act as his assistant in charge of the military railroads and telegraphs of the government and to organize a force of railway men. It was one of the most important departments of all at the beginning of the war.
(All three ANDYS leave. WORKERS take their places around scaffolds, as in scene 3, "Iron City." War noises mixed with machine noises. Slides of early etchings of armaments made in Pittsburgh. The following lines are in the nature of news bulletins.)

WORKER: Charles Knap's Fort Pitt Cannon Foundry, located at Twenty-eighth Street in Allegheny, furnished the army almost three thousand cannon.

WORKER: And ten million pounds of shot.

WORKER: And shell.

WORKER: The firm of Mason and Snowden was working on a third-class monitor early in 1861 even before Ericson's *Monitor* had its famous battle with the *Merrimac*.

WORKER: Congressman James Kennedy Moorhead's firm of Novelty Iron Works made a great deal of armorplate and constructed a million-dollar ironclad, the *Mentanomah*.

REPORTER: A gun was cast February first, 1864, in the presence of the inventor Major Rodman and other distinguished visitors. The gun in the rough weighed one hundred sixty thousand pounds, was twenty feet and three inches in length, with a twenty-inch bore, its maximum diameter being five feet and two inches.
(Explosions and Brady photo of Civil War dead. WORKERS *stare at the slide, then leave. The three* ANDYS *enter as a train puffing and chugging.)*

ANDY #1: There were so many delays on railroads in those days from burned or broken wooden bridges that I felt the day of wooden bridges must end soon. Cast iron bridges, I thought, ought to replace them,
(The three ANDYS *speak together.)*
so I organized a company,
(They shake hands.)
principally from railroad men. I knew how to make these iron bridges, and we called it the Keystone Bridge Company.

ANDY #2: I was always advising that our iron works should be extended and new developments made in connection with the manufacture of iron and steel, which I saw only in its infancy.

ANDY #3: Thirty-three and an income of fifty thousand dollars per annum. Beyond this never earn! Make no effort to increase fortune, but spend the surplus each year for benevolent purposes. Cast aside business forever.
(He goes off, deep in thought.)

ANDY #1: *(Holding a piece of rail.)* I had not failed to notice the growth of the Bessemer process. If this proved successful, I knew that iron was destined to give place to steel; and the Iron Age would pass away and the Steel Age take its place.
(Introducing him.)
Mr. Henry Bessemer.
(BESSEMER *enters and joins* ANDY #2. *Very British.* WILLIAM KELLY *enters.)*

KELLY: And Mr. William Kelly. Born in Pittsburgh in 1811. I discovered the pneumatic process.
(He joins ANDY #1.*)*

BESSEMER: I discovered the . . .

KELLY: So-called . . .

BESSEMER: Bessemer process.

KELLY AND BESSEMER: Of making iron into steel.

KELLY: I conceived the idea that, after the iron was melted, the use of fuel would be unnecessary; that the heat generated by the union of the oxygen of the air with the carbon of the metal, would be sufficent to accomplish the refining and decarbonizing of the iron to make steel.

BESSEMER: I fully succeeded in producing steel by simply forcing minute streams of cold atmospheric air upward through it for a space of fifteen minutes.

KELLY: I was the first inventor of this process now known as the Bessemer process.

BESSEMER: I could now see in my mind's eye, at a glance . . .
(He looks at CARNEGIE.*)*
the great iron industry of the world.
*(*ANDY #1 *leaves* KELLY *for* BESSEMER. BESSEMER *exits with* ANDYS #2 *and* #3, *one on each arm.)*

KELLY: *(Dejected.)* I was too poor, and I had to sell my patent. In looking back to the time when Mr. Bessemer's process and mine were made the subject of patents, I may observe that the loss of my patent left me without any share in the enormous royalties reaped from the success of our joint processes. In consequence of this, the world, true to itself, has done its best to ignore me and my process. The world shuns the man who does not get the money.
(He leaves.)

ANDY #2: *(Entering with* ANDY #1, *both wearing a sash of red, white, and blue.)* On my return from England, I built a plant for the Bessemer process of steelmaking; we called it the Edgar Thomson Steel Company. There, on the very field of Braddock's defeat, we began the erection of our steel-rail mills. During the excavating for the foundations, many relics of the battle were found—bayonets, swords, and the like.
(He shows a skull, ANDY #1 *a sword.)*

ANDYS #1 AND #2: The day of iron is past! Steel is king!
*(*ANDY #1 *waves his sword,* ANDY #2 *tosses away the skull. The stage is bathed in red, white, and blue light. A fanfare is sounded and intensely patriotic music continues until the end of the act. Enter* ANDY #3 *as Uncle Sam.)*

ANDYS #1 AND #2: The star-spangled Scotsman in a centennial salute to 1876!
(The three ANDYS *take a short march about the stage. Projection screens explode with stars, stripes, eagles, etc.)*

Act 1: Scene 7 / 39

(Title Slide: America, A Grand Historical Allegory by Bartley Campbell)

When announced by ANDY, *each of the following individuals marches on and assumes a picturesque pose—a tableau in the making.*

ANDY #3: Mechanics! Oh, the Mechanic, the mechanical engineer—a title of honor. Captain Bill Jones, manager of my Edgar Thomson works.
(Enter BILL JONES *carrying a huge red wrench.)*
It is the best to give the best for the masses, even in music, the highest of our gifts.
(Enter three of the STAGE BAND *costumed as the wounded trio of musicians from the familiar Revolutionary War painting.)*
We may look forward with hope to the day when it shall be the rule for the workman to be partner with Capital. 1876, the founding of the Amalgamated Association of Iron, Steel, and Tin Workers.
*(*WORKERS *enter, bearing an Amalgamated banner.)*
There is no class so intensely patriotic, so wildly devoted to the republic as the naturalized citizen and his child, for little does the native-born citizen know of the value of rights which have never been denied. The Immigrant.
*(*IMMIGRANTS *enter, wide-eyed.)*
Such fields of corn standing ungathered, such herds of cattle grazing at will. Agriculture.
*(*AGRICULTURE *enters holding a sheaf of wheat.)*
Plenty!
*(*PLENTY *enters holding a cornucopia.)*
Science!
(Enter BESSEMER.*)*
War! Peace!
(Enter LAFAYETTE *and a* WOMAN *crowned with laurels, with doves.)*
And Columbia!

(ANDY'S MOTHER *enters dressed as Columbia, bearing a torch. She is the center of the tableau.*)
The United States of America! 1876!
(*Exploding fireworks on projection screens. All wave flags and sing "America the Beautiful."*)

ENSEMBLE: (*Singing.*)
Oh beautiful for spacious skies,
For amber waves of grain.
For purple mountain majesties,
Above the fruited plain.
America! America! God shed his grace on thee,
And crown thy good with brotherhood,
From sea to shining sea!
(*Projections change from patriotic themes to images of blowing Bessemer converters and Pittsburgh skies afire. Smoke fills the stage.*)
Oh beautiful, for Pilgrim feet,
Whose stern impassioned stress
A thoroughfare for freedom beat
Across the wilderness.
America! America! God mend thine every flaw.
Confirm thy soul in self-control,
Thy liberty in law.
(*The singers burst into a fit of coughing, the tableau shatters, and all leave hurriedly.*)

(END OF ACT 1)

The basic stage for *Steel/City*.

An allegorical tableau represents the nation's centennial in 1876. Andrew Carnegie (Doug Farrell), the "Star-Spangled Scotsman," is at lower left.

Veronica, the "Sweetheart of the South Side," relaxes with steelworkers in a Soho tavern.

$400,000,000, the asking price for Carnegie Steel, causes the deal makers—all represented by U.S. Steel's first CEO, Judge Elbert Gary—to slump toward J.P. Morgan (right) for support.

Miss U.S. Steel (Jocelyn Johnson) prepares to lead the assembled steel magnates in song.

U.S. Steel, the world's first billion-dollar corporation, is represented by a billion-dollar bill bearing J.P. Morgan's portrait. Miss U.S. Steel (Jocelyn Johnson) leads her cohorts in song: "Her Dad's a Millionaire."

In a flashback from the pensioners' picnic, immigrants arrive in Pittsburgh against a backdrop of Pennsylvania Station.

Striking workers in 1919 listen to organizer William Z. Foster (William Wendt) under the guns of sheriff's deputies.

Act 2

Scene 1 / The Edgar Thomson Works

(Title slide: The Converting Department at the Edgar Thomson Works)

WORKERS *arrive in darkness through the audience. The sound of clanking tools. Stage is in the dimmest red light. On the rear screen: bubbling, molten metal. Imperceptibly, the "music" of the mill will start, will grow out of the rhythms of the* WORKERS *as they feed the works. They pickaxe the slag, throw bags of additives about, use wheelbarrows, carry buckets of water in yokes, shovel dirt, etc. They are dull and stolid, their movements expressive of great weariness. The sounds of the mill build to a deafening crescendo. The activity peaks, then the stage begins to clear. Above, on the scaffolds, the* PLANT MANAGER *enters, leading three or four* LADIES. *They wear hats of the 1880s period, goggles to protect their eyes, white gloves, perhaps work aprons to protect their clothing. The* MANAGER *beams with pride as he conducts the tour.* LADIES, *above on the "pulpit," stare wide-eyed at the half-naked* WORKERS *below them.*

MANAGER: The visitor to the converting department of the Edgar Thomson Steel Works finds himself almost dumb with amazement. In no other place hereabouts can be witnessed under one roof, so perfectly, the bondage of the elements—Fire, Air, and Water—or their complete subjection to the will of man.
(Oohs and aahs from the LADIES.*)*
This trinity of forces comes together in the converting house at Bessemer.

LADY #1: Bessemer parties are in constant process of formation, coming and going. . . .

LADY #2: And an evening scarcely goes by that does not witness a fair face in the pulpit—

42 / STEEL/CITY

MANAGER:—Surely a fitting accessory to a place where "converting" is done!
(Titters from the LADIES.*)*

LADY #2: A face lit up by the radiance of molten metal.

LADY #1: The pulpit, with its surrounding din, and its position in the very heart of the commotion and glare of the converters, is as familiar to the society belle of the Iron City as is the coziest, quietest nook in her boudoir.

LADY #3: As maid, wife, and matron, the Pittsburgh woman has witnessed the bowing of the converters.
(All smile and bow.)

MANAGER: There is not an industrial establishment in this country so favored by fair ones as the titanic laboratory of the Edgar Thomson works.
*(*LADIES *acknowledge the compliment. A fourth woman,* MISS MOORHEAD, *enters. She is more serious than the others, very young and beautiful. She stays somewhat apart from the others.)*

LADY #1: *(Identifying her.)* Miss Elizabeth Moorhead is one of the cotillion set. In addition to her social accomplishments, she has decided literary talent.
(During the following speech, lights dim out on all but MISS MOORHEAD.*)*

MISS MOORHEAD: *(Rather sadly, resignedly.)* I have no intention of writing about the development of industry in Pittsburgh and of its captains. My father's firm of Moorhead and Company has long since vanished from the Pittsburgh scene. On the rare occasions when my father took me to the cast-house, I was duly impressed by the amazing spectacle. But these expeditions were terrifying to me; there was something infernal about the roar of machinery, the columns of flame and smoke. I couldn't help feeling sorry for the men who were obliged to work, half-naked, in such an atmosphere of noise and fire. My attitude toward the great business of my native place was resignation rather than pride. It was necessary, this business. I knew that. Necessary that the rivers should be polluted, the once lovely hills gashed and torn, the whole city overhung with smoke. I accepted iron and steel as the background of my life, made no inquiries, understood nothing. It was . . . necessary.

(BLACKOUT)

Scene 2 / The Carnegie Bandwagon

(Title slide: Captain Bill Jones at the British Iron and Steel Institute, May 1881)

Lights up on CAPTAIN BILL JONES, *dressed in his Sunday best. He could be at a podium downstage. He carries a pointer.*

JONES: Now to the cause of the great output of American steelworks. On the introduction of the Bessemer process in America, quite a number of young men, who believed that the process would revolutionize the metallurgical world, became anxious to identify themselves with its development.
(A piercing whistle, followed by jazzy band music. CARNEGIE's *bandwagon sails onstage. It is an ornate, two-dimensional cut-out carried by the actors in front of them and bearing the inscription "Edgar Thomson Company." The* BAND *are a back-slapping rambunctious crew. As the bandwagon travels around the stage, each member is introduced with business suggested by the lines spoken by* BILL JONES. *Action should stop and start, shift from tableau to tableau, like lantern slides.)*

JONES: Shinn bossed the show; McCandless lent it dignity and standing; Phipps took in the pennies at the gate and kept the payroll down; Tom Carnegie kept everybody in good humor, with Dave Stewart as his understudy. And Andrew Carnegie? Oh, Andy looked after the advertising and drove the bandwagon!
*(*COLEMAN, KLOMAN, *and* SCOTT *remain quiet and apart from the others.* CARNEGIE, *played by* ANDY #3 *from act 1, pulls* SHINN *aside. The rest of the group square off in quaint, playful boxing poses. The following action in which they knock each other out happens very quickly.)*

CARNEGIE: *(Warmly.)* My partners are not only partners, but a band of devoted friends who never have a differ-

ence. I have never had to exercise my power, and of this I am very proud.
(To SHINN, *conspiratorially.)*
I want to buy Coleman out and hope to do so. Kloman will have to give up his interest.
*(*COLEMAN *and* KLOMAN *are knocked out.)*
It isn't likely McCandless, Scott, and Stewart will remain with us.
(Fight breaks out among them. TOM CARNEGIE *and* HARRY PHIPPS *cheer them on.* CARNEGIE *speaks privately to* SHINN.*)*
I scarcely think they can. I know Harry and Tom have agreed with me that you out of the entire lot would be wanted as a future partner.
*(*MCCANDLESS *and* STEWART *knock each other out, but* SCOTT *sneaks up behind* SHINN *and clubs him over the head.)*

SCOTT: In the month of September 1879, the Edgar Thomson Board met and accepted the resignation of Mr. Shinn. *(Whistle blows. Music. The bandwagon is reassembled with two* CARNEGIES, PHIPPS, STEWART, SCOTT, *and* MC-CANDLESS. *Sign now reads: "Carnegie Bros. and Company, Ltd." Bandwagon goes off with* ANDY *at the reins.)*

JONES: *(Who has been watching from the scaffolds, sarcastic.)* Next to the strong but pleasant rivalry of the young men who have assumed control of the works, another marked advantage which the American works have is the diversity of the nationality of the workmen.
*(*JONES *indicates with a pointer the homelands of different nationalities, as maps are projected on the screen.)*
We have representatives from England, Ireland, Scotland, Wales, and all parts of Germany; Swedes, Hungarians, and a few French and Italians; with a small percentage of colored workmen. Mixed with what I denominate "Buckwheats"—young American country boys—they make the most effective and tractable force

you can find. Welsh can be used in limited numbers. Scotsmen do very well, are honest and faithful.

(Crossfade lights to CARNEGIE; *bagpipes under his speech. He stands on the scaffolds beneath a slide photo of his first library.)*

CARNEGIE: Dunfermline, Scotland: my mother laid the foundation there of the first free library building I ever gave. Dunfermline named the building "Carnegie Library." The architect asked for my coat of arms. I informed him I had none, but suggested that above the door there might be carved a rising sun shedding its rays with the motto: "Let there be light."

(BLACKOUT)

Scene 3 / Initiation Ritual of Amalgamated Association of Iron, Steel, and Tin Workers

(Title slide: Initiation)

Enter in the blackout unionized WORKERS, *with their* PRESIDENT *and a young* INITIATE, *holding candles. They arrange themselves around the scaffolds. The* PRESIDENT *is played by same actor who played* MATTHEWS. *The* INITIATE *is the* WORKER *later killed during the Homestead Strike (scene 7).*

PRESIDENT: Brothers, we are about to open this lodge of fraternally united Iron, Steel, and Tin Workers, for the purpose of considering such measures as will tend to perpetuate our organization.
(Chorus of ayes.)

VICE-PRESIDENT: *(Addressing* INITIATE.*)* Will you obey all the laws and rules of this organization, they not conflicting with the duties you owe your family, your church, or your country?

INITIATE: I will.

PRESIDENT: You further promise that you will always regard and treat every worthy member of this organization as a brother, and that you will do all in your power to procure employment for such brothers as may desire situations, in preference to any and all nonunion men?

INITIATE: I will.

VICE-PRESIDENT: Let caution be engraved deeply in your heart. You must be watchful of all you say and do, especially in the presence of our enemies, and, as you value your manhood and your honor, avoid all talk and controversy about the internal workings of this lodge outside of this room.

(INITIATE *nods vigorously.* WORKERS *come forward and greet the new member. He and three or four others go, with much good-natured banter, to a boardinghouse, the Greasy Spoon.)*

Scene 4 / The Greasy Spoon

(Title slide: The Greasy Spoon)

The boardinghouse is projected on the rear screen. On stage, only a long dining table and eight chairs, four occupied by huge men.

JAMES DAVIS: *(Played by actor who was the* PUDDLER.*)* Our boardinghouse, the "Greasy Spoon." Our landlady is Irish, and her motto is—

LANDLADY: *(Heavy accent.)* If there's any fightin' to be done, I'll do it myself.
(She places a huge platter of food before the men. A scramble.)

LANDLADY: Stop yer fightin' before I hack yer hands off.

DAVIS: The "Greasy Spoon" isn't an appetizing name, but it is meant as a lure to men who live by muscular toil. It sounded good to us millworkers, for, like Eskimos, we craved fat in our diet. We are great muscular machines, and fat is the fuel for our engines.
(Grunts of satisfaction as the MEN *tackle great gobs of fatty meat.)*
Then one of those reformers came to live with us for a while at the "Greasy Spoon."
(A slender, gentle, friendly fellow joins the table.)

REFORMER: So much grease in your food will kill you.

DAVIS: All we knew is that our stomachs cried for plenty of fat.
(The MEN *eat noisily.)*

REFORMER: Your landlady feeds you fat because it is the cheapest food she can buy. Milk, eggs, vegetables, and fruits would cost more.
(To audience.)

That greedy woman is lining her pockets at the expense of your lives.

DAVIS: The landlady's kindly, and she took the reformer's advice. She banished the fat pork, and supplied the table with . . .

LANDLADY: *(Removing meat and serving a new menu.)* Spinach . . . milk . . . fruit . . .
(The REFORMER eats heartily. The MEN eat sparingly.

DAVIS: *The men, losing energy, slump over the table as he speaks.)* We ate this reformed food and found we were growing weaker every day at the puddling furnace. We became sullen. Gradually all laughter ceased in the boarding house. We even felt too low to fight.
(Faint stirrings from the MEN; then low grumbles; finally shouts of "Hog fat!" "Pork!" "Plenty of pork!" "Grease!" etc. They attack the REFORMER and throw him out. They clear the stage and proceed jovially to the Gay Nineties Club.)

Scene 5 / The Gay Nineties Club

(Title slide: The Gay Nineties Club)

As the WORKERS *walk from the Greasy Spoon, piano music is heard, a placard is hung out,* WOMEN *appear, and we are at the Gay Nineties Club. The Amalgamated's* PRESIDENT, VICE-PRESIDENT, *and the* INITIATE *are engaged in earnest conversation.*

PRESIDENT: Machinery at the Edgar Thomson works in 1885 displaced fifty-seven of sixty-nine men on the heating furnace.

VICE-PRESIDENT: They started bringing in large numbers of immigrants in order to keep wages low and conditions unfavorable for organizing.

PRESIDENT: Swedes were brought in from the East.
(They have settled in at the club, where the revelry now overcomes their serious conversation.)

DRINKER: You can't kill a Swede.

ANOTHER DRINKER: *(Fondling a* WOMAN.*)* You can't crowd out a Welshman.

ANOTHER: And you can't beat the Irish!

MASTER OF CEREMONIES: *(Mockingly.)* And now, ladies and gentlemen,
(Disclaimers from the assembled.)
Veronica, our "Sweetheart of the South Side," singing "Soho on Saturday Night."

VERONICA: *(Singing.)*
They tell us in Soho on Saturday night
Most every person you meet they are tight,
The men with their bottles, their wives with a can,

The young girls go prowlin' around like a man.
One woman I met, I'll never forget,
She fell in a sewer and she got soakin' wet.
The crowd gathered round her, all thinkin' her dead
But then she got up—and here's what she said:

CHORUS:
Oh, isn't it queer how some women drink beer?
They drink and they drink and get tight.
And the new license plan, it ain't worth a damn
In Soho on Saturday night.

VERONICA:
Oh, they all tossed the drinks,
Mister Carnegie did the same.
As fast as they could fill them up,
Around the drinks they came.
Mister Frick got blind drunk,
Mister Carnegie couldn't see,
I was bad, but Mister Frick
Was a damned sight worse than me.

CHORUS:
Oh, the new license plan, it ain't worth a damn
In Soho on Saturday night.

VERONICA:
You see them in Soho on Saturday night;
Women and men drink with all of their might,
And when they have finished the booze in one place,
They go to the next bar. It's such a disgrace!
One fellow I knew, he got in a stew,
He woke up next morning in the Highland Park zoo.
The animals thought that the fellow was dead,
But then he got up, and here's what he said:

CHORUS:
Oh, isn't it queer how some fellows drink beer?
They drink and they drink and get tight.

And the new license plan, it ain't worth a damn
In Soho on Saturday night.
In Soho on Saturday night.

Scene 6 / Prelude to Homestead

Same setting. As VERONICA *takes her bows, a husky* WORKER *has stalked silently into the club. His face and clothes are covered with soot and grime, and he crushes a newspaper in his hand. His intensity silences the* CROWD. *He speaks in a low, passionate voice.*

WORKER: Carnegie Brothers and Company propose a *reduction* in the scale of the men employed on the hundred-nineteen-inch plate mill. A *reduction* in the thirty-two-inch slabbing mill and in the open hearth departments. *(The club empties.* UNION BROTHERS *gather around the* WORKER. *One takes the newspaper from him.)*

UNION BROTHER #1: *(Reading from the paper.)* The scale should be in force for one year and six months, terminating January first instead of midsummer.

UNION BROTHER #2: Aye, that's fine, isn't it? We'd be negotiating then in January and out on strike in the freezing cold.
*(*FRICK *has entered across the stage from the union group.* CARNEGIE *follows.)*

UNION BROTHER #1: Henry Clay Frick has declared war on the unions.
(Slide of FRICK. *Union group watches* FRICK *and* CARNEGIE.*)*

FRICK: After the twenty-fourth of June, 1892, we do not propose to deal with the Amalgamated Association.

CARNEGIE: *(Impatiently.)* The vast majority of our workers are nonunion.

FRICK: *(Insistently.)* The mills have never been able to turn out the product they should, owing to being held back by the Amalgamated men. When these workmen refused to make terms with us, we concluded it would be necessary to protect our own property and secure new workmen.

CARNEGIE: *(Admonishing him.)* There is an unwritten law: "Thou shalt not take thy neighbor's job." The employer of labor will find it much more to his interest to allow his works to remain idle and await the result of a dispute than to employ a class of men that can be induced to take the place of other men who have stopped work. Roll a large lot of steel plates ahead, which can be finished, should the works be stopped for a time.
(Determined.)
The Homestead works will be nonunion after the expiration of the present agreement.
(CARNEGIE and FRICK leave.)

MCLUCKIE: *(Played by one of the actors already identified as an organizer.)* We were persuaded to vote the Republican ticket four years ago. . . . Vote for high tariffs and you get high fences, Pinkerton detectives, thugs, and militia.

CROWD: *(Gathered to hear MCLUCKIE.)* Shut down the mill! Down with Frick! Strike!
(The WORKERS sing the "Strike Song.")

VERSE:
We are asking one another,
As we pass the time of day,
Why working men resort to arms
To get their proper pay.
And why our labor unions
They must not be recognized
Whilst the actions of a syndicate
Must not be criticized.
Now, the troubles down at Homestead
Were brought about this way,
When a grasping corporation
Had the audacity to say:
"You must all renounce your union
And forswear your liberty,
And we will give you a chance
To live and die in slavery."

CHORUS:
> Now, the man that fights for honor, none can blame him;
> May luck attend wherever he may roam.
> And no son of his will ever live to shame him
> Whilst liberty and honor rule our home.

VERSE:
> Now, this sturdy band of working men
> Started out at the break of day,
> Determination in their faces,
> Which plainly meant to say:
> "No one can come and take our homes
> For which we have toiled so long,
> No one can come and take our place—
> No, here's where we belong!"
> A woman with a rifle
> Saw her husband in the crowd,
> She handed him the weapon
> And they cheered her long and loud.
> He kissed her and said,
> "Mary, you go home till we're through."
> She answered, "No, if you must fight,
> My place is here with you."

CHORUS:
> Now, the man that fights for honor, none can blame him;
> May luck attend wherever he may roam.
> And no son of his will ever live to shame him
> Whilst liberty and honor rule our home.
> (CROWD *exits noisily, shouting "Strike!"* ALEXANDER BERKMAN *appears in an isolated spot. Slide of* BERKMAN.)

BERKMAN: My name is Alexander Berkman. I was born in the province of Vilna, Russia, in 1867. I came to New York at nineteen. Later I obtained a position in the Singer Sewing Machine factory in Elizabeth. I joined the Penkert Nihilists. I am a disciple and lover of the notorious Emma Goldman.
(GOLDMAN *comes and takes his hand.*)

GOLDMAN: We are professed anarchists. We are violent and destructive opponents of all government.

BERKMAN: *(Holding up book.)* Johann Most's "Science of Revolutionary Warfare."
(He packs his bag.)

GOLDMAN: Sasha's experiments took place at night when everybody was asleep. While Sasha worked, I kept watch. I lived in dread every moment for Sasha, for our friends in the flat, the children, and the rest of the tenants. What if anything should go wrong?—but, then, did not the end justify the means? Our end was the sacred cause of the oppressed and exploited people. . . . What if a few should have to perish?—the many would be made free and could live in beauty and comfort.

TOGETHER: We swear to dedicate ourselves to the cause in some supreme deed, to die together if necessary, or to continue to live and work for the idea for which one of us might have to give his life.
(He snaps his bag shut.)

(LIGHTS DOWN)

Scene 7 / The Homestead Steel Strike

(Title slide: The Homestead Steel Strike)

WORKERS *enter from one side of the stage, managers from the other. Lights up on* FRICK, *at his desk.* WORKERS *in the shadows.*

FRICK: We today are turned out of our plant at Homestead and have been since the first of July. There is nobody in the mills up there now; there is simply a mass of idle machinery and nobody to look after it.
(Writing.)
My dear Mr. Pinkerton, we shall want three hundred guards for service at our Homestead mills as a measure of precaution against interference with our plan to start operation of the works on July eighth, 1892.

PINKERTON: *(Entering,* FRICK's *letter in hand.)* Since the strikes of '77, my agencies have been busily employed by great railway, manufacturing, and other corporations for the purpose of bringing the leaders and instigators of strikes to the punishment they so richly deserve. Hundreds have been punished. Hundreds more will be punished.

FRICK: *(Shaking* PINKERTON's *hand.)* The only trouble we anticipate is that an attempt will be made to prevent our men from going to work, and possibly some demonstration of violence upon the part of those whose places have been filled.

HUGH O'DONNELL: *(As lights come up, he addresses his* LIEUTENANTS.*)* The committee has decided to organize their forces on a truly military basis. The force of four thousand men has been divided into three divisions or watches; each of these divisions is to devote eight hours of the twenty-four to the task of watching the plant.

FRICK: *(To* PINKERTON.*)* Your guards should be assembled at Ashtabula, Ohio, no later than the morning of July fifth, when they may be taken by train to McKees Rocks, transferred to boats, and landed within the enclosures of our premises at Homestead.

O'DONNELL: During their hours of duty, these appointed captains will have personal charge of the most important posts—the riverfront, the water gates and pumps, the railway stations, and the main gates of the plant.

FRICK: We think absolute secrecy essential in the movement of these men, so that no demonstration can be made while they are en route.

O'DONNELL: In addition to all this, there will be held in reserve a force of eight hundred Slavs and Hungarians. The brigade of foreigners will be under the command of two of their kinsmen.
(The stage has become quiet and tense. Lights are dim. UNION MEN *have set up their outposts, and management has left the stage. A long, mournful whistle is heard, and the Pinkerton barge, represented by a rolling platform, advances from upstage.)*

WORKERS: *(Whispering.)* The Pinkertons are coming! The Pinkertons are coming!
(The whisper builds to a cry. WORKERS *scurry over scaffolds, readying themselves.* WOMEN *accompany them with clubs.)*

DEPUTY NORDRUM: We are Pinkerton detectives. We were sent here to take possession of this property and to guard it for the company.
(Dim up a slide of Homestead Steel Works.)

WORKER: Don't let the black sheep land!
(A shot rings out. PINKERTONS *take cover.)*

NORDRUM: *(Knocking aside a cocked rifle of one of his* MEN.*)* It's no use returning the fire until some of us are hurt.
(The PINKERTONS *put out a gangplank. One of the* WORKERS *runs to the gangplank and lies flat upon it to block the path of* OFFICER HEINDE, *who attempts to shove him aside.)*

NORDRUM: Now listen, we are taking over the works and we advise you to disperse.

WORKER: Don't step off that boat!
(Prone WORKER *draws revolver and shoots* HEINDE *in the thigh. Firing breaks out. Prone* WORKER *is shot; so is another,* MARTIN MURRAY, *the union* INITIATE *from scenes 3 and 5. He falls in a downstage area.)*

WORKER: *(Crouching over* MURRAY, *and brandishing a rifle.)* Men of Homestead, fellow strikers! Our brothers have been shot down before our eyes by hired thugs. We must kill them!
(Another volley of shots. CROWD *surges to barge.* HEINDE, *atop barge, waves a white flag.)*

HEINDE: *(Desperate and in great pain, to one of his* MEN.*)* I don't feel like lying here and bleeding to death.

O'DONNELL: *(Climbing the scaffold to place himself between the mob and the* PINKERTONS.*)* This is enough of the killing!
(To PINKERTONS.*)*
On what terms do you wish to capitulate?

COOPER: *(A* PINKERTON.*)* On the assurance that there will be no violence toward the men, and that you will give us free passage from Homestead.

O'DONNELL: *(To* CROWD.*)* Agreed?
(The CROWD *reluctantly assents.* O'DONNELL *addresses the audience.)*
When all was ready, I gave the order, and they marched

out, and I remained on the boat until the last man.
(He is silhouetted against the screen).
I will state by this time the people were coming up, down and across the river, and that the barges were in the hands of the rabble.

WOMAN: *(As the* PINKERTONS *are debarking.)* You have killed two men this morning! I saw you!
(She attacks one of the PINKERTONS. *Pandemonium breaks loose. The* PINKERTONS *run a gauntlet and are beaten and abused, spit upon.* O'DONNELL *watches helplessly.)*

O'DONNELL: The Pinkertons were subjected to very inhuman treatment, which our men were powerless to protect them from. That night, we sent them off.

ORGANIZER: When the Pinkerton men came, the Homestead steelworkers saw a mob of men with guns coming to take their jobs, to take away their chance to work, to break up their homes. . . .
(Several of the WORKERS *shoulder the dead body of the* INITIATE.*)*

REVEREND MCILYAR: This town is bathed in tears today, and it is all brought about by one man, who is less respected by the laboring people than any other employer in the world.
(Indicating FRICK, *on whom the lights come up.)*
There is no more sensibility in that man than in a toad.
*(*STRIKERS *freeze in a tableau.)*

FRICK: *(Writing at his desk.)* July eighteenth, 1892. Men of Homestead. We invite you to return to your old positions. *(Almost heartily.)*
Work to commence at the usual time.

WORKER: Not a soul returned.
(Light out on FRICK.*)*

BERKMAN: *(He emerges from the* CROWD *of strikers, who leave.)*
The time for speech was past. Throughout the land, the toilers echoed the defiance of the men of Homestead. The steelworkers had rallied bravely to the defense; the murderous Pinkertons were driven from the city. But loudly called the blood of Mammon's victims from the banks of the Monongahela. Loudly it calls. It is the people calling. Ah, the People! The grand, mysterious, yet so near and real people.
(More calmly.)
Frick is the responsible factor in this crime. I will kill Frick, and of course I shall be condemned to death.
(Light out on BERKMAN. *Lights up on* CARNEGIE, *on scaffolding beneath a projection of Skibo Castle.)*

CARNEGIE: *(The sounds of a Scottish air in the background.)*
I was traveling in the Highlands of Scotland when the trouble arose, and did not hear of it till two days after. I received the following cable from the officers of the union of our workmen: "Kind master, tell us what you wish us to do and we will do it for you." This was most touching, but— alas—too late. The mischief was done. The works were in the hands of the governor.
(A REPORTER *approaches him.)*

REPORTER: *(With a British accent.)* Do you have anything to say concerning the troubles at your mills?

CARNEGIE: I have nothing whatever to say. I have given up all active control of the business and I do not care to interfere in any way with the present management's conduct of this affair.

REPORTER: But you must have some opinion in the matter.

CARNEGIE: The handling of the case on the part of the management has my full approval and sanction. Further than this, I have no disposition to say anything.
(The REPORTER *leaves.* CARNEGIE *dictates a telegram.)*

To Frick:
(Light upon FRICK *at his desk, attended by his assistant,* LEISHMAN.*)*
All anxiety gone since you stand firm. Never employ one of these rioters. Let grass grow over the works. Must not fail now. Stand firm—law and order—wish I could support you in any form.
(Changing his tone.)
To my partner, George Lauder: Matters at home *bad.* Still, we must keep quiet and support Frick and those at the seat of war. Frick cabled yesterday that Homestead had started slowly.
(In disbelief.)
He thinks we'll soon win. We shall win, of course, but we may have to shut down for months.
(Impatient.)
Schwab should be sent to Homestead; *he* manages men well. Have suggested this to Frick. . . .
(Cross fade to BERKMAN *approaching* FRICK'*s office.)*

BERKMAN: July twenty-first, 1892. I called twice at Mr. Frick's office on the second floor of the *Chronicle-Telegraph* office. I got as far as the anteroom. The presence of callers there . . .

LEISHMAN: I'm sorry. Mr. Frick will not be able to see you for a few minutes.

BERKMAN: I left. Returned at two.
(He knocks LEISHMAN *down and rushes into* FRICK'*s office.)*
Frick! I draw my revolver. Raise the weapon. Frick attempts to rise. I aim at the head.
(A shot.)
Frick on his knees, his head against the arm of the chair. Dead?
*(*LEISHMAN *jumps on him as he is about to shoot again. They struggle, a second shot hits* FRICK *in the neck. A*

third goes into the ceiling. BERKMAN *is pinned into a chair by* LEISHMAN *and* FRICK. *He draws a knife and stabs* FRICK *in the thigh. A* WORKER *enters and picks up* BERKMAN'*s gun and is about to shoot him.*)

WORKER: Mr. Frick, do you identify this man as your assailant?

FRICK: Don't shoot; leave him to the law. But raise his head and let me see his face.

BERKMAN: I have lost my glasses.

WORKER: You'll be damned lucky if you don't lose your head.

FRICK: Don't kill him, I tell you. Let the law take its course.

BERKMAN: *(As he is dragged off.)* I have lost my glasses.

LEISHMAN: Before the day's work was finished, Frick made the following statement to the press.

FRICK: This incident will not change the attitude of the Carnegie Steel Company toward the Amalgamated Association. I do not think I shall die, but if I do or not the company will pursue the same policy, and it will win.
(Pause.)
Send this to Andrew Carnegie.
(Lights go up on CARNEGIE. FRICK *dictates a telegram.)*
There is no necessity for you to come home. I am still in shape to fight the battle out.
(To LEISHMAN.*)*
I will never recognize the union, never, never! If Mr. Carnegie interferes, every manager that he has will resign, and of course I will get out of the concern. But I do not think he will interfere.

CARNEGIE: Silence is best.
(Lights dim down on CARNEGIE *and up on* STRIKERS, *who enter bearing the body of* MURRAY *(formerly the* INITIATE*).*

Throughout the following exchange lights crossfade between STRIKERS *and* FRICK.)

LEISHMAN: *(Showing a newspaper to* FRICK.) July. "Union Leaders under Indictment."

THREE ORGANIZERS: Not guilty . . . not guilty . . . not guilty. . . .

MCLUCKIE: I had a good rest in jail.

LEISHMAN: August. We made five heats last night and the steel was the prettiest I ever saw.

O'DONNELL: Simply let the Carnegie Company recognize the Amalgamated Association by reopening the conference doors. . . .

LEISHMAN: *(Showing a newspaper to* FRICK, *and reading aloud.)* September. *The Christian Advocate:* "This is no time to arbitrate. The battle of law and order must be fought to the end."

FRICK: October. The firmness with which these strikers hold on is surprising to everyone.

ORGANIZER: November. The great Homestead strike is finally dying out.

ORGANIZER: In humanity's name, the press appeals for aid for suffering Homestead. Pride seals the lips of starving men and women.

FRICK: November 21, to Andrew Carnegie in Florence, Italy. Strike officially declared off yesterday. Our victory is now complete and most gratifying. Do not think we will ever have any serious labor trouble again.
(Crossfade to CARNEGIE.)

CARNEGIE: *(Under slide projection showing a scene in Florence.)* Life worth living again. First happy morning since July. Surprising how pretty Italia. . . . Congratulate all

around—improve works—go ahead—clear track—shake.
(Dim out on CARNEGIE.*)*

ORGANIZER: *(Bitterly.)* If you want to talk in Homestead, you must talk to yourself.
(A bell begins to toll. It continues under a dirge sung by the STRIKERS. *Dim up on rear screen a slide of a fallen worker.)*

CHORUS: *(Singing.)*
As I leave, sweet mother, don't cry for me, Mother, for me.
And, poor heart of mine, don't break, poor heart,
Don't break as I go to a new land.

I will go, I will go to America, I go to my fortune in America.
Please don't cry, don't cry, my mother, my mother.
I must go to my fortune.

What good? What good do I find in America? What good in America?
No work in America, no work in America.
How I miss my homeland.
(Lights dim as WORKERS *exeunt with* MURRAY'*s body on their shoulders—a somber funeral procession.)*

Scene 8 / The Philosophy of Wealth

(Title slide: Philosophy—Herbert Spencer, Andrew Carnegie, and Russell Conwell.)

The sound of organ music, very syrupy. A slide of stained-glass windows projected on the rear screen. CARNEGIE *and philosopher* HERBERT SPENCER *are seated on a bench.*

CARNEGIE: No pangs remain of any wound received in my business career save that of Homestead. It was so unnecessary. The men were so outrageously wrong.

SPENCER: *(Solicitous.)* It seems hard that a laborer incapacitated by sickness from competing with his stronger fellows should have to bear the resulting privations. It seems hard that widows and orphans should be left to struggle for life or death. Nevertheless, when regarded not separately but in connection with the interests of the universal humanity, these hard fatalities are seen to be full of beneficence, the same beneficence which brings to early graves the children of diseased parents.

CARNEGIE: The survival of the fittest. . . . The race has been allowed to develop in freedom; hence, while still savage, the stronger physically were the foremost.
(Acknowledging his philosopher friend.)
And later, under civilization, the strongest mentally have become the leaders.

SPENCER: *(Modestly brushing off the compliment.)* Under the natural order of things, society is constantly excreting its unhealthy, imbecile, slow, vacilating, faithless members in order to leave room for the competent ones entitled to reward.
(Lights up on REVEREND RUSSELL CONWELL, *above, who sermonizes.)*

CONWELL: Some people have said to me: "Don't you sympathize with the poor people?" Of course, I do . . . but the number of poor who are to be sympathized with is very small. To sympathize with a man whom God has punished for his sins, thus to help him when God would still continue a just punishment, is to do wrong; no doubt about it. Let us remember that there is not a poor person in the United States who was not made poor by his own shortcomings, or by the shortcomings of someone else. It is all wrong to be poor, anyhow.

SPENCER: Fostering the good-for-nothing at the expense of the good is an extreme cruelty.

CARNEGIE: It were better that the millions of the rich were thrown into the sea than to foster the drunken, the slothful, and unworthy.

CONWELL: The man who get the largest salary can do the most good with the power that is furnished him. The love of money is the root of all evil, not the money itself.

CARNEGIE: The day is not far distant when the millionaire will become the trustee and agent for his poorer brethren, entrusted for a season with the increased wealth of the community and bringing to their service his superior wisdom, experience, and ability to administer.

CONWELL: To secure wealth is an honorable ambition. I say that you ought to get rich, and it is your duty to get rich.

CARNEGIE: Thus, in these principles, I believe we've been quoting from the true gospel of wealth! . . . adherence to which will solve the problems of the rich and poor, hasten the coming brotherhood of mankind, and at last make our earth a heaven.
(Music swells. CARNEGIE *and* SPENCER *leave. Light fades on* CONWELL *as his hand traces in the air the sign of the dollar.)*

(BLACKOUT)

Scene 9 / Twilight of the Gods

(Title slide: Götterdämmerung)

The stage is dark. The following scene is played with echo-amplified voices and with the figures of CARNEGIE *and* FRICK *silhouetted against and behind the rear projection screen. They move and gesture exaggeratedly.*

FRICK: Mr. Carnegie, it is time we considered the reorganization of the Carnegie Steel Company and its consolidation with the H. C. Frick Coke Company.

CARNEGIE: *(Brightly.)* Good morning, Mr. Frick! What would you say to a two-year contract on coke at a dollar thirty-five a ton?

FRICK: *(Taken aback.)* Why should you insist on fixing the price of coke at cost? The value of our coke properties has been at every opportunity depreciated by you and Mr. Lauder.

CARNEGIE: We never had friction before; it annoys me more than dollars.

FRICK: The Frick Coke Company has always been used as a convenience by the Carnegie Steel Company.

CARNEGIE: *(To audience.)* When I could not bring my associates in business to my views by reason, I have never wished to do so by force.

FRICK: *(To audience.)* I have no desire to raise trouble in the organization, but, in justice to myself, I could not say less than I have.

CARNEGIE: *(Apoplectic.)* Frick must resign! If he doesn't get out voluntarily, I'll kick him out!
*(*CARNEGIE *boots* FRICK *out of screen image.)*

(BLACKOUT)

Scene 10 / Consolidation Scene

(Title slide: A Meeting of the Board)

A whistle blows and the bandwagon, bearing the placard "Carnegie Steel Company," comes onstage, with FRICK *at the head. Riders include* SCHWAB, SINGER, PEACOCK, PHIPPS, CLEMSON, LAUDER, BOPE, GAYLEY, LOVEJOY. *Music until* LOVEJOY *speaks. Lights up full. They climb off the wagon, seat themselves at tables set in a V, with* FRICK *at the apex, upstage.* CARNEGIE *is on an upstage platform, silhouetted against a slide of downtown Pittsburgh at the turn of the century. All but* FRICK *are puppets with handlebar moustaches wearing bowler hats;* CARNEGIE *pulls the strings. It is winter.*

LOVEJOY: *(Played by the actor who was the* CRIER *in act 1.)* At a meeting of the Board of Managers of the Carnegie Steel Company, Ltd., Pittsburgh, Pa., twelve-thirty p.m., Monday, January sixteenth, 1899, there were present Messrs. Frick (chairman), Singer, Schwab (president), Peacock, Phipps, Clemson, Lovejoy, Lauder, Gayley, Bope.
(Each nods as his name is called. Two nod on Bope.)

SHWAB: *(Taking his cue from* CARNEGIE.*)* Would like Board to approve approximately $500,000 expenditure for purchase of Bethlehem Plate Mills.

BOARD: *(At* CARNEGIE'*s cue, mechanically.)* So moved. Aye.

SCHWAB: The demand for open hearth, as opposed to Bessemer, steel is increasing each day. A careful calculation would indicate that ten additional furnaces are necessary for the Homestead Steel Works.
(Slide: Belching smokestacks from Homestead mill.)

PHIPPS: Move $1,300,000 appropriation.

FRICK: That cost appears high.

(As he is about to continue, LAUDER, CARNEGIE's *kinsman, cuts him off at* CARNEGIE's *signal.)*

LAUDER: *(With a Scots burr.)* It is the right thing to do.

BOARD: So moved. Aye.

PHIPPS: Move $218,000 for improvements at our Carrie furnaces.

LAUDER: It is the right thing to do.

BOARD: So moved. Aye.
(Content that the meeting is going to his satisfaction, CARNEGIE *leaves.)*

PEACOCK: The new steel car combination has approached us on the subject of a contract, and would be willing to buy probably a thousand tons of steel per day, provided . . . (BOARD *leans eagerly toward* PEACOCK.)
we stay out of the steel car business.

FRICK: *(The force of his personality tugging the* BOARD *in his direction.)* I am strongly in favor of going ahead with the plans for our new car works. I would like to ask Mr. Peacock if he is selling much material today.

PEACOCK: We have nothing to sell but structural material, on which we are getting good prices. We have under consideration a contract with the American Tin Plate Company of New Jersey.

LOVEJOY: *(Reading the contract rapidly, slowing only to emphasize the clauses in restraint of trade. While* LOVEJOY *reads,* SCHWAB *rises and stands next to* FRICK, *whispering in his ear.)* One hundred twenty-five gross tons . . . cash on the twentieth of each month. . . . Sellers agree so long as the buyers perform their part of this contract, they will not sell to any competitor tin or black plate bars of the kind covered in this contract . . . and the sellers agree . . .

(BOARD *leans toward* LOVEJOY.)
not to enter in competition with the Carnegie Steel Company, Limited, in any of the products which the steel company manufactures.

SCHWAB: *(The* BOARD *leans toward him with ears cocked.)* Mr. Carnegie is en route to Pittsburgh and will be at the office this morning. Nothing could be done with him looking toward a reconciliation. I did my best.
(The BOARD *leap as one from the table and form a receiving line for* CARNEGIE, *just entering.)*

(Slide of Carnegie with his board of directors.)

*(*CARNEGIE *hands a document to* SCHWAB.*)*

SCHWAB: *(Reading aloud to* FRICK.*)* Dear Sir, I beg to advise you that pursuant to the terms of the so-called Iron-Clad Agreement and at the request of the Board of Managers, I have today delivered to the Carnegie Steel Company a transfer of your interest in the capital of said company. Yours truly, C. M. Schwab.
*(*SCHWAB *retreats in embarrassment to join the* BOARD.*)*

FRICK: *(Advances on* CARNEGIE, *who is perhaps sitting in a tippable swivel chair.)* Harmony is so essential for the success of any organization that I have withstood a great many insults from Mr. Carnegie in the past, but I will submit to no further insults in the future.
(He flips CARNEGIE *backwards, seizes him by the ankles, and shakes him until money drops from his pockets.)*

CARNEGIE: *(Upside down.)* Frick is a man disposed to make a personal matter out of every difference of opinion.
(He scuttles upstage, his men dusting him off.)
At times, moreover, he gives way to violent outbursts of passion.

FRICK: *(Bowing upstage; sarcastic.)* Gentlemen, I beg to present my resignation as a member of your board.

(To audience; a spot picks him up.)
Settlement made. I get what is due me. All well. It is not my intention to be officially connected with the re-organized concern.
(Calling upstage.)
Carnegie! You being in control, stockholders and public look to you to see that the great Carnegie Steel Company is managed successfully and honestly. You cannot trust many by whom you are surrounded to give you facts.
(CARNEGIE's men should be melting into darkness, whistling with feigned nonchalance the bandwagon theme. CARNEGIE follows them.)
Do not let them hide things from you. You are being outgeneraled all along the line, and your management of the company has become an object of jest.
(Blackout on FRICK. On comes a stately parade of "businessmen" led by J. P. MORGAN and JUDGE GARY. All are played by the women of the company.)

(Title slide: A Billion-Dollar Deal)

(Each actress carries a photo-placard of JUDGE GARY before her face—except for J. P. MORGAN, whose placard bears MORGAN's own portrait—and smokes a cigar. Music—the CARNEGIE bandwagon theme played at a slower speed—until they seat themselves at the tables formerly occupied by CARNEGIE's people.)

MORGAN: *(At one end of tables.)* Judge Gary.
(Echoes of "Judge Gary" from the others.)

JUDGE GARY: *(At head of table, bowing.)* Federal Steel Company.
(He then introduces the others at the table, who nod in response.)
"National Tube." "American Bridge." "National Steel." "American Tin Plate." "American Steel Hoop Company." "American Steel and Wire." "American Sheet Steel Com-

pany." "Lake Superior Consolidated Iron Mines." "Oliver Iron Mining." Messrs. J. P. Morgan and Company are considering plans for the acquisition of the properties of some of the largest iron and steel companies of this country. There will be such ownership or control as to secure perfect and permanent harmony in the larger lines of this industry. It is not, however, intended to obtain control of any line of business or to create any monopoly or trust, *(Snickers and chuckles and clouds of smoke from behind the placards.)* or in any way antagonize any principle or policy of the law.

MORGAN: The entire plan of organization and management of the United States Steel Corporation shall be determined by J. P. Morgan and Company.
(The shrill whistle of CARNEGIE's *bandwagon cuts him off. Music brings* CARNEGIE *on upstage platform.)*

JUDGE GARY: *(In response to worried and angry murmurs from behind the placards.)* Now, if we can buy the Carnegie Steel Company . . .

MORGAN: *(Brooding.)* I don't believe I could raise the money.
(Lights down on all but MORGAN, *who remains in a spot. Crossfade to* CARNEGIE, SCHWAB, *and* CHARLES R. FLINT—*the last being a photo-placard—discovered on upstage platform.)*

CARNEGIE: *(To* SCHWAB, *but said for the ears of* FLINT, MORGAN's *cohort.)* How much cheaper, Charlie, can you make tubes than the National Company?

SCHWAB: Ten dollars a ton.

CARNEGIE: *(The fire of battle in his eyes.)* Go on and build the plant.
(Groans from MORGAN's *people.)*
If it is a fight they want, here we are always ready. Here

is a historic situation for the managers to study Richelieu's advice. "First, all means to conciliate; then, all means to crush."
(Worried murmurs from MORGAN *and company.)*
In the case of this Tin Plate Company, as in the case of the American Wire Company, if our president . . .
(Grasping SCHWAB *by the elbow.)*
steps forward and informs these people that we do not propose to be injured. . . .
*(*SCHWAB *nods his understanding and departs, to be discovered later at* MORGAN's *table.)*

FLINT: Carnegie spent several hours describing to me his plans for increasing his production and fabrication of steel.

CARNEGIE: *(In deep conversation with* FLINT.*)* . . . To establish an extensive pipe and tube manufacturing plant, representing an investment of twelve million dollars.

FLINT: . . . A structural steel to undersell the American Bridge Company.
(Reaction from MORGAN *and company.)*

CARNEGIE: Spend dividends for a hoop and cotton-tie mill, for wire and nail mills, for lines of boats. . . .

FLINT: *(To audience.)* I cannot explain why Carnegie gave me so much detailed information about his business.
(It dawns on him.)
Knowing my pleasant relations with J. P. Morgan and Company, he may have shrewdly divined that I was gathering information in their interest.
*(*CARNEGIE *chuckles.)*

CARNEGIE: *(Calling after* FLINT, *who is headed toward* MORGAN.*)* What I have talked to you about is a matter of national interest, and you are free to repeat anything I have said.
*(*CARNEGIE *chuckles.* FLINT *goes to* MORGAN. *Crossfade to*

76 / STEEL/CITY

tables, as CARNEGIE *remains in spot.* FLINT *whispers in* MORGAN's *ear.)*

MORGAN: Mr. Schwab.

SCHWAB: *(Rising from a place of concealment behind the phalanx of placards.)* I would like to speak about the advantages of doing business of a larger scale than has been attempted.
(Photo-placards lean to SCHWAB *and envelop him. When he is uncovered,* SCHWAB *has become a photo—one of* MORGAN's *men.)*

MORGAN: *(Photo-placards lean over to* MORGAN *as he speaks. He pauses after "If.")* If . . . you can get Carnegie to sell, I will undertake the matter.

SCHWAB: *(Trotting over to the foot of the upstage platform, from which* CARNEGIE *surveys the scene.)* Mr. Carnegie?
*(*CARNEGIE *chuckles. Says nothing, but scrawls a figure on a piece of paper and drops it into* SCHWAB's *hand. All screens explode into dollar signs and figures: $400,000,000.)*

MORGAN: Four hundred million dollars!
(Weakly.)
I accept.
(Music brings on the male company as the CARNEGIE *bandwagon, which—now a part of U.S. Steel—carries photo-placards of* JUDGE GARY, *first chairman of the board. The stage is flooded with images of* GARY's *face. All march in formation and then form a solid "wall" of placards—with* MORGAN *in the center—facing the audience.* CARNEGIE *and* MISS U.S. STEEL *step out from behind the wall, she identified by a banner worn across her body in beauty-contest fashion. Just before she sings, the actors reverse the photo-placards to display a billion-dollar bill with* MORGAN's *face at the center. It is inscribed as a certificate of the U.S. Steel Corporation. As* MISS U.S. STEEL *sings,* CARNEGIE *tosses money into the air and into the*

audience; slide projections show the mansions of steel millionaires and the slums where Pittsburgh millworkers live.)

MISS U.S. STEEL: *(Singing.)*
I've finally found the place where I belong!
My dad's a millionaire!
The fortune's come we've waited for so long,
And I'm a millionaire!
I vow I'll wear these ragged clothes no more,
Here take them, bub, and pitch them out the door,
I'll have the best, the finest in the store,
Since dad's a millionaire!

MALE CHORUS:
Hurrah! Hurrah! Now sing a rousing song,

FEMALE CHORUS:
Goodbye! Goodbye! to poverty and care.

MALE CHORUS:
The fortune's come she's waited for so long.

ALL:
Her dad's a millionaire.

MISS U.S. STEEL:
So now I know this shack will never do,
Since Dad's a millionaire!
He'll build a house with indoor bathrooms too,
'Cause he's a millionaire!
I vow I'll never sit out in the cold,
I've had a life of miseries untold,
I'll sit inside, on toilet seats of gold,
Since dad's a millionaire!

MALE CHORUS:
Hurrah! Hurrah! Now sing a rousing song.

FEMALE CHORUS:
Goodbye! Goodbye! to poverty and care.

MALE CHORUS:
> The fortune's come she's waited for so long.

ALL:
> Her dad's a millionaire.

MISS U.S. STEEL:
> I'll eat the best and richest foods by far,

FEMALE CHORUS:
> Since dad's a millionaire!

MISS U.S. STEEL:
> I'll dine on steak and even caviar,

MALE CHORUS:
> 'Cause dad's a millionaire!

MISS U.S. STEEL:
> I vow I'll never eat another meal,
> Unless it's served on china that is real,
> Our silverware, the finest U.S. Steel,

ALL:
> Since dad's a millionaire!

MALE CHORUS:
> Hurrah! Hurrah! Now sing a rousing song.

FEMALE CHORUS:
> Good-bye! Good-bye! to poverty and care.

MISS U.S. STEEL:
> The fortune's come . . .

ALL:
> She's waited for so long,
> Her dad's a millionaire!
> Her dad's a millionaire!

(END OF ACT 2)

Act 3

Summer 1975

The setting is a farm meadow dotted with trees. On the screens, a leafy background with Pittsburgh's skyline barely visible in the distance. Picnic tables are scattered about. Retired STEELWORKERS *and their* WIVES *play at horseshoes, poker, and checkers; prepare and serve food (sandwiches, perhaps ethnic specialties like stuffed cabbage and kolbassi); and draw beer from a keg. At times, the action flashes back to incidents from former times, as suggested by recollections of the* PICNICKERS. *The* STAGE BAND *plays ethnic instruments both at the picnic and during the musical flashbacks. Before the lights go up, a murmur of voices (excerpted from the taped oral histories of which most of the act's dialogue is composed) is heard indistinctly in the darkness. These fade into the onstage voices of the actors, some of whom are discovered, while others drift in during the scene.*

ANTOINETTE: I was born and raised and we didn't have no boards in the floor, just the hard-packed dirt.

PHILOMENA: My father died, I was only seven years old. At times they were discouraged. They would remember the farms and how green everything was. South Side at that time was always dirty. It was discouraging after living on a farm and coming to that.

MIKE ZAHORSKY: My father come from East Slovakia, which was part of Austria-Hungary at that time. They were all considered Hungarians, and that's where they got that derogatory term "Hunkies."

PAUL JAKIELA: My dad—the only thing he knew in the way of machines was the wheel, that was it.

80 / STEEL/CITY

ANTOINETTE: They say then that in America the fences are plated with kolbassi.
(Laughter.)

RUDY: Well, they came over here because it was a new country, you know, more or less . . . better living conditions. . . .

WALTER: *(Winning a hand at poker.)* Pot of gold.

MIKE ZAHORSKY: They come over for economic reasons.

RUDY: To make their livelihood. . . .

MARY MUSHALKO: *(Putting tablecloths on picnic tables.)* My mother and father were from Siedliska, Poland. My dad was a happy-go-lucky farmer. He didn't have to work. The women done the work. My dad didn't want to come here. Because he heard that when people come here they have to work. So all the way on the ship when he was comin' in, he cried. The whole time that they was comin', he was cryin'.

MIKE ZAHORSKY: The way my father came to America was the way in which ninety-nine percent of the people came—you came to a relative, a friend, or an acquaintance.

MARY MUSHALKO: My dad always said he wished he were a bird and he would fly right back to Poland.
(Laughter.)

ANTOINETTE: They claimed the water was better there.

MARY: My sister was not quite fourteen when she came here. And I'll never forget that day, because I seen her coming down the tracks where the Christy Park works are now, there in McKeesport. And I seen her coming with this bundle, and she had a shawl on, and I'm running in the house and I'm telling my mother, "There's Gypsies coming! There's Gypsies coming!" And she run out, and here it was my sister.

MIKE ZAHORSKY: *(Stepping downstage, while the lights dim*

on the picnic.) When my mother come over here, she come over with a bundle on her back—that was her entire dowry. I remember later, we went to the Pennsylvania Station, and there would be a train arrive there . . .

(Title Slide: Pennsylvania Station, Pittsburgh)

(YOUNG WOMEN *begin to appear, carrying bundles.)*
And you would see eight or ten of these young ladies come in, maybe sixteen to nineteen, because after nineteen you was already off the market. And all these men were lined up to see which one had the biggest bundle and which looked the best.
(Men eye the YOUNG WOMEN, *make tentative advances. The music starts and a simple courting dance is performed, in Old World style. Slides of children at play in the slums. The couples go off together, the* WOMEN *cradling the bundles as if they were babies. Lights fade back up on picnic.)*

ALL: "Ten kids." "The women worked like slaves." "Don't know how they did it." "No washers, no dryers." "And no plumbing." "Fifteen cents an hour." "They all had big families."

MIKE ZAHORSKY: This old friend has illustrated one of these old Slovak women—he says, you know, "One at the arm, one at the tit, one in the corner covered with shit." So that tells you something as to how close those kids came. *(Laughter.)*

RUDY: Today they have this and they have that . . .

FRANK: Everybody pitched in then to help one another. Neighbors.

RUDY: Conditions in them days was totally different.

MIKE ZAHORSKY: In those days there were empty fields near here, and there were cows and we had milk.

PATRICIA MAGDIK: We have garden place in Brentwood. Way up hill. We have potatoes, tomatoes, watermelons; nobody steal it like they do this time; nobody take it; nobody watch it, anyhow.

KATHERINE PELLEGRINO: I remember when they had the bake ovens outside, made out of bricks. They'd bake these great big loaves of bread and the ladies, they'd put these breads on their head, they'd walk like this with those big big huge loaves of bread. Italian women.

PATRICIA MAGDIK: My place was never empty of people. We had company every day. Not company. Stay—like home. Eat like home. Feel like home. I like that.

MIKE ZAHORSKY: We had events in the home. For instance, there were a lot of christenings. There were weddings. St. Joseph's Day, all the Josephs would get together and throw a party. St. Michael's Day, all the Michaels would get together and throw a party. Every name's day. I'm Slovak, and we used to observe about eight Italian holidays a year.
(They laugh.)

ANTOINETTE: Their religion was holding people together.

MARY MUSHALKO: At that time, none of those people knew what it was to separate. The women, no matter how the men treat her . . . they never left.

ANOTOINETTE: They never left.
(Pause.)
Because there was no place to go.

MARY MUSHALKO: And then they didn't have mothers and fathers here, that they could run home to mother. And there weren't that many jobs for the women to get, either. At that time for the women, that was a crime if you had to go to work.
(Reaction from ensemble; some agree, some disagree.)

MORAVIAN WOMAN: *(Feisty.)* Nobody ever don't say that women don't work in America. I have lived here a long time in McKeesport, Pa. I have kept boarders ever since I came here, and I haven't had time to sit in a rocking chair, and my husband never bought me any candy. It's true, you can't beat us women here, as you could in the old country. Soon after we came here, my husband beat me when he was drunk. I carried a black eye for a week. Then the young girl who takes the money at the grocery store asked me how I hurt myself. I said, "I didn't hurt myself, my husband did it." Then that young girl said, "You tell me the next time he hits you." It wasn't long before he beat me again, and I told her, and the police came and took him by the neck and put him in the lockup, and it cost me twenty-five dollars to get him out. *(Guffaws and teasing remarks from the* MEN; *groans from the* WOMEN.*)*
I earned that money myself, and it was no punishment to him. I told the young woman about it, and she said: "The next time he hits you, you hit back." I said, "Is it allowed?" She laughed, and said: "If he hits you first and you kill him, nothing will happen to you." It wasn't long until he came home drunk and beat me again, and I gave him one with the rolling pin and he fell, and as he was lying there I got so angry I gave him another and another, and after that he knew better than to beat me.
(Laughter. Another WOMAN *brings on a big plate of food. Everyone gathers around.)*

MARY MUSHALKO: *(As she speaks the lights dim; the* PICNICKERS *become the* BOARDERS *spoken of by* MARY MUSHALKO.*)* My dad, when he came here, it was about 1904, and at that time they were just starting to come in. A lot of single fellows were comin' in. My mother—she had a seven-room house which they rented, and they had about eighteen boarders. When one half worked, the other half sleeps. My mother, she was up at two o'clock in

the morning washing clothes. And then at five they went to milk cows. She done everything she possibly could to make that home a happy home. Come spring, they would move whatever furniture they had, and if they had any sort of congoleum on the floor, they rolled that up, and they used to put soap on the floor,
(Two young MEN *pantomime soaping the floor.)*
and they would dance. There was a lot of fellas. They danced sometimes all night.
(An ensemble performs an exciting ethnic folk dance—perhaps Polish or Yugoslavian—accompanied by singers and music of the tamburitza and other ethnic stringed instruments. MARY *gets caught up in it, and briefly we sense her youth. When the dance ends, the couples leave and light slowly comes up on the picnic.* MARY *sighs.)*
And my mother had eighteen boarders; and would you believe it, each one bought his own food, 'cause each one was saving their money to go back to Poland. They would buy their soup meat—like, if she was making soup, vegetable soup, well, each one would have a string on their part of the meat. One ate more, one ate less. One bought a half a pound, one bought a pound, and they had it marked with strings. And then they had these lunch buckets, and she had to get up at four o'clock in the morning. And when me and my brother were big enough, we had to wash them lunch buckets—eighteen of them every day.

SAM DAVICH: *(As picnic food is being served.)* In those days, if you was fortunate enough to be able to buy a lunch bucket and bring it, you needed it to keep away the rats. The mill, it was infested with rats at that time.

MIKE ZAHORSKY: You had no cooling or anything.

MIKE #2: If you had a ham in there, it mighta turned green.

SAM DAVICH: That's right.
(They laugh.)

FRANK: No, you'd hang your lunch on a rope suspended from the ceiling so the rats wouldn't get it.
(General assent.)

FRANK: But here we are, Sam, talking to one another right now, and we survived. I got a heart condition, you got one too. He come out and smelled the fresh air, we all smelt the fresh air and started takin' heart attacks.

STEVE KIKA: You know, this environmental control—they talk about it so much, right? Now, down along the Monongahela, you had the old Bessemer converter, you had the open hearth blowin' up that coal—every house on the South Side burned wood or coal, whatever they had to burn—and all those people lived to be a ripe old age of eighty, eighty-five.

MIKE #2: What you're saying is there's something about that dirty air that makes you live longer?

STEVE KIKA: That's right, Mike.
(All laugh and dispute him.)

MIKE: You come outa the mill and you couldn't see it. You'd get home, you'd blow your nose and it'd be black in the hanky. You'd come home with a black collar.

STEVE KIKA: You'd come home like an Indian.

BERNARD GORCZYCA: My dad wore a leather apron and threw pigs into the furnace. He'd wash out in the yard, they had a hydrant there, they didn't have a pump.

MIKE ZAHORSKY: My father was fifty-six years old when he died. He was a grinder in a specialty steel mill. And the place where these people worked, there was no provisions to suck out this dust and dirt. Particles of high-carbon steel. They inhaled that. My father liked to drink. Ninety percent of these people liked to drink. I learned later that the only relief he got was when he took that drink. It sort of loosened up that spitum, and he would spit up this

hard stuff, but it was the consistency of grease. And these people died, and nobody said anything about it.
(Pause.)

ROY MCCHESTER: The main item was trying to stay alive. There wasn't no safety.
(Pause.)

PAUL JAKIELA: *(Bitterly.)* J. & L. was known as the Butcher Shop. As a matter of fact, they had a ward on the South Side Hospital which was exclusively J. & L.'s. You had no safety, as we know safety now. Production, production, and profits, that is all they were interested in. You were dispensable.

MIKE ZAHORSKY: I never had no problems workin' with J. & L.; we've come a long way since them days.
(JAKIELA and ZAHORSKY are about to argue when RUDY changes the subject.)

RUDY: In them days, throughout the mill you had mules.

MIKE #2: In them days, if that mule broke his leg or something, you'd get fired. They could kill a man over there. That was nothin'. But it cost you a lot of money to buy a mule.

STEVE KIKA: It ain't like in the movies where a man falls in a vat of steel, a ladle of steel, and they bury that.

SAM DAVICH: They don't bury that goddamn thing.

FRANK: Where you gonna bury two hundred and fifty tons of steel? . . . no way.

ALL: Nah—no—I never heard of that.
(Laughter, but with an edge to it.)

STEVE KIKA: *(Bitterly.)* Sanitation gang. They called it the crippled gang. When a man got injured on the job, they'd put him on a lower job and also cut his pay. I wasn't bitter over the pay. I just couldnt go anywhere.
(Pause.)

PAUL JAKIELA: There was no pensions.
(Pause.)

ROY MCCHESTER: A strong back and a weak mind, that's all you needed.
(Pause.)

PAUL JAKIELA: My dad worked ten, twelve hours a day, seven days a week, and they asked him to work on Easter Sunday. My dad says no, he wants to spend that one day with the family. So the boss told him, If you don't work Easter Sunday, you don't come out Easter Monday.
(JAKIELA curses under his breath.)

ANGELO ROSSANO: We had nothing here. All we had was a company town and a bunch of stool pigeons. In that day, you had to keep your mouth shut. You were not a free man in that day, because the company controlled the mills. The company controlled Aliquippa. You had to be a good jackass to do a good job. Without a union, a man was lost.

STEVE KIKA: I remember, the A. F. of L. sent in an organizer around the Pittsburgh area. We had to meet secretly in private homes, but we did have a place on Market and Fifth, way up on the fifth floor. This was 1919.
(The CROWD stirs, remembering.)

ALL: *(Various voices.)* Yes. I remember that. 1919.
(Lights begin to dim.)

KIKA: *(To audience.)* We tried to have a big mass meeting. These coal and iron police come in there, we call them Cossacks. They rode right in where the meeting was, it was packed with men, women, and children. Them horses were trained to bite. They'd go in and grab you just like a mad dog. 1919. Works were down in some places. . . .

(Lights have dimmed. Slides of Russian Cossacks on horseback.)

88 / STEEL/CITY

(Title Slide: The Great Steel Strike of 1919.)

PICKNICKERS *have become* STRIKERS, *led by* JOHN FITZPATRICK *and* WILLIAM Z. FOSTER, *who addresses a massive crowd. A* REPORTER *is on the fringes. This flashback should have the feel of a Living Newspaper.*

FOSTER: *(Played by the actor who plays* JAKIELA.*)* The National Committee for Organizing Iron and Steel Workers is now seeking to get higher wages, shorter hours, and better working conditions from the steel companies. Are you willing to back them up to the extent of stopping work, should the companies refuse to concede these demands?

ALL: *(Various voices, cheering.)* Yes! Slovensi? Polski? Ya?
(Cheer.)
Ruski? Da?
(Cheer.)
Italiani? Si?
(Cheer. WORKERS *begin to form a picket line and walk in a circle, carrying placards reading: "Eight-Hour Day," "One Day's Rest in Seven," etc. Slide of a closed mill gate on rear screen.)*

FITZPATRICK: *(Handing out signs.)* The twenty-four international unions in the steel industry and affiliated with the A. F. of L. have decided by unanimous vote to cease work Monday, September twenty-second, 1919.

REPORTER: Chairman Fitzpatrick, Judge Gary of U.S. Steel says that not more than ten to fifteen percent of the men will quit work.
(Slide of JUDGE GARY, *as pictured on placards in act 2.)*

FITZPATRICK: If Judge Gary is right, then we're a lot of damn fools. We have been organizing for several months and are in good shape.

REPORTER: *(To audience.)* In anticipation of the steel strike,

what do we see? In the Pittsburgh district, thousands of deputy sheriffs have been recruited at several of the largest plants. The Pennsylvania State Constabulary has been concentrated at the commanding points. It is as though the preparations were made for an actual war.
(The upstage platform rolls forward. On it are SHERIFFS' DEPUTIES *arranged to recall the opening image of the Homestead Strike scene.)*

FOSTER: *(Pulling* FITZPATRICK *aside and indicating two of the armed* MEN.*)* Sheriff William F. Haddock of Allegheny County and his brother, supervisor of the American Sheet and Tin Plate plant.

FITZPATRICK: Haddock told the newspapers:

HADDOCK: This is America, and its my observation that ninety percent of the offenders against the law in matters of this kind are either aliens or of foreign extraction.
(Slides of headlines: GERMAN DESIGNS SUSPECTED—Gazette-Times, Oct. 3; INSPIRED WALKOUT TO REGAIN TRADE, STEEL MAN ASSERTS—Chronicle-Telegraph, Oct. 2.)

FOSTER: From the first, these Pittsburgh papers were violently antagonistic to the steelworkers.

DEPUTY: *(Taunting the* WORKERS, *as do the others.)* The steel strike can't win!
(The CROWD *ignores the taunts.)*

FOSTER: They played up the race issue.

DEPUTIES: Europe's not what it used to be! Maybe the doors of the old U.S.A. won't open again!
(The CROWD *reacts angrily.)*

FOSTER: Full-page advertisements!
(Slide: Chronicle-Telegraph, Oct. 6: An advertisement proclaiming "Go back to work" in seven languages.)

DEPUTIES: America is calling you! Be a hundred-percent American! The steel strike can't win, boys! Workers flock back to jobs!
(As these cries are heard, slides of headlines flash in quick succession: WORKERS FLOCK BACK TO JOBS. BRADDOCK REPORTS THREE TIMES AS MANY WORKING TODAY AS YESTERDAY. REPORT LABORERS GOING BACK ALL THROUGH DISTRICT. STRIKE CRUMBLING STEEL MEN SAY.—*Leader, Sept. 25; Chronicle-Telegraph, Sept. 27, Oct. 1.)*

WORKER: *(Picking up a newspaper hurled down by a* SHERIFF.*)* Report laborers going back all through district.
*(*CROWD *grumbles, is confused.* FOSTER *and* FITZPATRICK *go to them, re-form their picket line, rally their spirits.)*

FOSTER: This is an organized journalistic effort to stampede the men back to work. Sixty thousand workers in the Pittsburgh district are out!
*(*STRIKERS *are restored to order. During the following speeches, they cry out their slogans defiantly.)*

WORKER'S WIFE: *(To* FOSTER.*)* We'll have to move from here . . . They'll never take him back after the strike.

WORKER: One day's rest in seven!

WIFE: He'll be blacklisted. You don't know what they make you suffer for being a union man in a town like this.

WORKER: Eight-hour day!

WIFE: They talk about the Cossacks, but it's the spies that's bad. There is always someone watching. There's a free country for you. I tell you, there's no such thing for a union man in a steel town.

DEPUTIES: There's no good American reason for the strike! America will never stand for the red rule of bolshevism! Bolsheviks!! Revolutionaires! Hunkies!

(Angry denials from CROWD. *A huge* WORKER *strides out, seizes a* DEPUTY, *and attempts to throttle him.)*

WORKER: *(After being restrained by the* CROWD.*)* For why we fought the war? For why we bought Liberty Bonds? For mills? No! For freedom and America—for everybody. No more work like horse and wagon. For eight-hour day!
(The CROWD *is on the verge of violence, but their attention is diverted by a number of* SCABS, *guarded by a* DEPUTY. *The* DEPUTIES *part the* CROWD *to let the* SCABS *through. Slide changes to a mill belching smoke.)*

ALL: *(Various voices.)* "Don't go in the mill!" "Scabs!" "Don't take our jobs!" "What's going on?" etc.

FOSTER: *(Apart, to* FITZPATRICK.*)* The foreigner comes over here, and he seems to respond to an appeal better than the Americans do. He will stick, while the American will go back to work. That is what happened in the mills just now.
(Slides: 8,000 JOHNSTOWN STEEL STRIKERS RETURN TO WORK. 10,000 CAMBRIA STEEL MEN RETURN—Chronicle-Telegraph, Nov. 17; Post, Nov. 19. The CROWD *is beginning to break. Picket signs are going down.)*

WORKER: *(To* FOSTER.*)* How do you think the strike go? You think we goin' to win now pretty soon?
(Before FOSTER *can answer, another* WORKER *pulls him aside.)*

WORKER: I got four boys. I want they shouldn't have to work fourteen hours a night and ten hours light. We all feel like that, but when we see how many Americans went back to work as soon as mill is opened, we Slovaks feel like we was out skating and the ice cracks, and we look around and only us, everybody else goes ashore.
(Pause.)

But we got to win, just the same—sometime.
(Slide: "Go Back to Work" in seven languages fills all screens. The stage empties but for FOSTER.*)*

FOSTER: When the Hunkies tell me they were let down, I know it. Their ranks were never really broken. The only way to beat them was to starve them out. The Big Men of Labor never gave the movement the essential moral and financial backing. When Mike Tighe, president of the Amalgamated, ordered back his men at a plant near Cleveland, it started an avalanche.
(Alone in a pin spot, a newspaper clutched in his hand.)
The jails swarmed with arrested strikers—especially in the Soho district of Pittsburgh, where the main entrances of the National Tube Works and the J. & L. plants are.
(Bitterly.)
And now come the Pittsburgh papers with the story that Police Commissioner Peter P. Walsh has made application to be retired from the Pittsburgh police force on half pay, in order that he might accept the appointment as chief of the mill police of the J. & L. Company.
(Pause.)
When a Labor Committee demanded that Mayor Babcock of Pittsburgh investigate the situation, the honorable gentleman refused. He admitted that the action of the steel companies was ill-advised; however, the matter was now past . . . history.
(As light blacks out on him, he crumples the paper and tosses it away. Dim up on picnic.)

ALL: *(Various voices.)* 1919! You got locked in the mill. Cossacks and the Hunkies! Amalgamated back off. No money.

ANTON CINDRICH: The company, it imported scabs, mostly blacks at that time. They come up from the South.

FREEMAN PATTON: *(Angrily.)* How could my father be in

sympathy with the strike? What did he know about the strike, what did he know about unionism? West Virginians, Polish, Hungarians, anything Caucasian got into the union, but no blacks. All my dad knew was work. Anything that deprived you of your work he hated. Hunkies got in the unions, but no blacks.

WALTER KLIS: *(Reacting to* PATTON *and advancing on him.)* I was called a Hunky a number of times. In those days, I did resent it. I'd tell a guy off, I didn't care who he was.

ROBERT MILANOVICH: *(Stepping between* PATTON *and* KLIS, *changing the subject.)* If you didn't know how to fight, you didn't go out to play.
*(*KLIS *and* PATTON *disengage.)*

JOHN MAGDIK: They should have sunk all the boats bringing Hungarians over here. *(To his wife.)* Then I wouldn't of had to put up with you.
(Laughter from the MEN.*)*

MARY MAGDIK: The best thing you done in your life—you was nothing until you married a Hungarian!
(Loud laughter from the WOMEN.*)*

DAVICH: The majority was Serbian, Croatian, and Polish down in the blooming mills.

PAUL JAKIELA: The Germans came here before the Poles did. In fact, I know friends who said that it was to our advantage to learn a few words in German. Things opened up for you in a little better way than the others.

MIKE ZAHORSKY: The Irish had charge of the melting department in this little steel company that I worked. Flatdie jobs were in the hands of the Swedes. These were the big Swedes. How they would yodel through the mill!
(He yodels badly.)

WALTER KLIS: I worked in a rolling mill. The Slav descent,

they always had the rough jobs. Between them and the colored, you had to use a lot of muscle. Once in a while you'd find one man or two that would pass halfway up that ladder. But they never got the top job of a roller or a supervisor.

FREEMAN PATTON: *(Agreeing.)* I worked at the Clairton coke works. The working force was black and Mexican. Whites were top foremen. This white guy would come in. He would start at gap inspector. He didn't know the first thing—he'd never seen a coke plant in his life. They would take that fella to me. I would teach him how to be my boss. I'd train him, and maybe in six months he's become a battery foreman. Now they are paying him more money for letting me teach him how to be my boss than they are me for teaching him. That would frustrate me every now and then.
(Many speak. PATTON *is silent.)*

PHILOMENA: We went to school with the black children. But you didn't think of them as black. They were just one of the kids in school. You swam with them.
(Innocently.)
Of course, they never thought of intermarrying or anything. . . .
(PATTON *looks at her. Some of the* PICNICKERS *are embarrassed.)*

THELMA HENRY: *(Coming to the rescue.)* Right down by the water plant on Fifteenth Street, we had a beautiful pool and playground. There used to be the little foreigners, and we had a melting pot down in there. And we all played together. It was a lot of fun back then. At that time, the Third Ward here in McKeesport was considered a very nice ward. Mostly Christian people lived in it. We got along fine, fine. The children played together. The parents visited each other. It really was just beautiful.
(A slow blues starts in background. Lights have dimmed

on picnic area. THELMA HENRY *improvises a blues song about her old neighborhood, and about the dirty, backbreaking work in the mills. Lights slowly dim up on picnic area through next speech.)*

THELMA HENRY: Pickling the tin, you had to work in a lot of acid. That's why they had to wear the aprons and boots. I think the pickling mills had a lot to do with my husband's condition. Working in a lot of acid. And they had no protection.

MCCHESTER: That was during the Depression.
(Pause.)

KAY KLUZ: Nothing could be as rotten as the Depression. There wasn't any living to make. Five, six, seven days a week you would come to work. You would cluster around a given portion of the mill, a station, and the foreman would come and look at you and say, "You, you, you, and you. You work today—the rest of you go home." "Shall I come to work tomorrow, John?" "Take a chance, there might be something for you." Then after a while you recognize: "Why are these three men, or two men chosen and not me? Why?" And you walked out of the mill. You walked with the men who were rejected. And you learn from walking with these guys and going home and talking with them; and you learn: "Keep your mouth shut, don't let them see what is on your face. Be nice to this guy. Be nice to that guy." So what made us band together? Misery. We wanted a system of things. All we wanted was "It's your turn today. It's my turn tomorrow." We kind of felt that the concept of fairness meant more than accidents over which we had no control. And we learned very quickly that out of this rejection we had to protect each other. Men getting together. Men sharing misery. This did it!
(Buzz of assent from PICNICKERS.*)*

MIKE ZAHORSKY: I'll never forget that big day in Pittsburgh when they had forty-three thousand people in Forbes Field listening to Roosevelt, and he told us, "You're going to have this right to organize." And the people went back, they went back to their various organizations and companies, and they didn't forget that.
(Loud agreement.)

JOSEPH ODORCICH: In those days it was the Holy Three: God, Roosevelt, and John L. Lewis.
(Laughter.)

JOSEPH WIATRAK: *(Sarcastically.)* We had what we call the company unions.

MIKE ZAHORSKY: The Employment Representation Plan.

WIATRAK: There was no representation.

MIKE ZAHORSKY: The industry got together and they are going to give these people a chance to organize their union. "Why should you have some coal miner with big eyebrows come in here and tell you how to run your union? Why should you have some guy come in from the coal fields, who don't know shit from shinola, and tell you, and tell you how you should live?" And so forth and so on. "We are going to give you a union," they said, "but first of all we are going to throw a big picnic. . . ." Unlimited expense to keep the union out.

JOE CENTONI: In them days, anyone who was a union man was a radical. They called you other names—Communists—everything. Even if you don't know what it was, they used to call you—Communists.

ODORCICH: *(As the musicians tune up.)* There's no question we had Communists and we used them. They're a hell of a people for rabble-rousin'; they had a lot of guts in those days. The plant I worked, we had signed up over four hundred guys. The plant was owned by a guy named C. S.

Cokes. Now, he used to made a tour in the plant ten o'clock in the morning.
(Mimes Cokes giving his employees a close look.)
The strategy was, we're gonna meet out on the floor and talk to him about havin' a union. Five of us temporary officers, we grabbed ahold of Mr. Cokes, and the temporary president says, "We want to talk to you about a union." Old Mr. Cokes, he blew his stack.
(Chuckling at the memory and playing Mr. Cokes.)
Called us Communists, called us everything under the sun. He told us to get the hell out of his plant. He was gonna go out and get the cops.
(Pause.)
"Well," we said, "O.K., Mr. Cokes, you don't wanna talk to us, fine, your plant's on strike." So we gave the right signals and the boys dropped their tools and everybody started heading for the door. He says, "Wait a minute, wait a minute!"
(Waving his hands, rushing after the men to bring them back.)
"Let's talk about this thing." He says, "Come up to my office." We went up to his office and he started out by jumpin' on us and raisin' hell. He says, "How do I know you guys have the men organized?" I had all the cards in a shopping bag. I says to him, "Would you like to count the cards?" So I opened up the shopping bag and dumped it on his desk, and I said: "Count 'em!" Two days later, we signed a document that said we had a union.
(Laughter, a cheer or two. Amid the jubilation, one of the MEN *prods* ZAHORSKY *into singing a song, "Aja Lejber Man.")*

MIKE ZAHORSKY: *(Singing.)*
I'm a labor man, I work every day.
To myself I figure, are my savings bigger?
Or should I try to save some more pay?
(He then changes to Slovakian.)

Aja lejber man, Robim Kazdi den,
Vse sebe rahujem, kelo zosporujem
Kelo zosporujem natidzen?
(The dancers assemble and dance while the chorus sings.)

CHORUS:
Pride petnasti, ta i sesnasti,
talara nabaru, "dajnam po poharu,
naj se napijeme napedu."

Skraju list dostal, bim daco poslal,
sednem za stolicek, napisem listocek,
poslem zene stovku napedu.
(After the dance, the weariness of the day descends on the PICNICKERS. They fan themselves and drain their glasses. They begin to pack away their food, baskets, etc.)

PHILOMENA: We used to have dances in the hall of the church every Saturday. The grownups and the younger ones.

MARY MUSHALKO: Before, the families were closer together.

PHILOMENA: It's simple things, simple things.
(The PICNICKERS are leaving now, shaking hands, embracing, carrying out baskets and jugs.)

MARY MUSHALKO: When we were children, what my family enjoyed, my mother would sit there and maybe sing songs, or they would tell us all these creepy stories that they had back in Poland.

STEVE KIKA: Well, take back forty, fifty, sixty years. You was young, you was walking around, you was in your prime. You believed the doors was open. You'd go to a picnic at Kennywood Park. You'd sleep on the floor in the summer; you didn't have no air conditioning. You'd let the wind blow.
(He goes out. Pause.)

MIKE ZAHORSKY: We, our fathers and us, went out to start

these unions. We felt that we were creating a sweeter piece of bread for our children. The young man today, it's hard to tell him that we retirees worked forty years before we got one week's vacation.

WALTER KLIS: I liked to work. I liked the feel of being able to throw that steel around. Oh, hell, we was throwin' around twenty tons. You take a little piece of steel and you stretch it out for a hundred and twenty, a hundred and fifty yards. You prided yourself in how efficiently you could do it. Somebody would make a mistake on a piece of steel, and you would be able to correct them. You had that comradeship.

MIKE ZAHORSKY: I have an old fellow, he is close to eighty-five years old. He was my helper in the blacksmith shop twenty-three years. As soon as we meet, regardless of who may be there, he gets tears in his eyes and he says, "You know, more like twenty-three years I work for you, Mike Zahorsky, no one time you say son-of-a-bitch, no one time you give me hell." He says, "All the time we work together, all the time we makin' good. Mike, I never forget you tell me when we makin' some kind of job, 'Pile 'em up nice, Steve, 'cause if you pile 'em like potatoes, nobody pay any attention to 'em.'" Pride in your work. Sweep off the platform. You have to take pride in your work from the beginning to the finish. You know, this man taught me something. He couldn't read or write to sign his name. The foreman said, "You dig this ditch, Stever, you dig it twenty-four inches wide and two feet deep, from here to there." He got a two-by-four and measured it off. And when he was done, he stepped back—he smiled, how beautiful the ditch was dug. Who the hell do you ever find talking about a beautiful dug ditch?
(He goes out.)

PAUL JAKIELA: The old timers, they made you think why you should be acknowledged as a human being. Nowadays, one crane comes in with about three hundred thousand pounds of scrap, dumps it into the ladle. That one backs away, another crane comes in with a hundred forty thousand pounds of molten metal. In twenty-five minutes the whistle blows to prepare for tap.

WALTER KLIS: In other words, human beings working down in the mills will be more or less robots.

PAUL JAKIELA: *(Agreeing.)* I'm talkin' now of two hundred fifty tons of metal. When my dad worked at J. & L., it took them twelve to fourteen hours with small open hearths to make the same amount.

WALTER KLIS: When I was president of local 1272 on the South Side, we had fifty-five hundred men. Twenty years ago they dropped down to forty-four hundred. Last ten years we've gone down to twenty-seven hundred.
(He goes out.)

PAUL JAKIELA: Rubber, plastic, glass. Twenty-five or thirty years ago, did you ever have a fork or knife that was made out of plastic?
(He breaks the utensil he is holding. He says goodbye to the others and goes out.)

FREEMAN PATTON: I tell the children: first you got to visualize, then after you visualize you got to organize, then after you organize you got to deputize, then after you deputize you got to supervise, then you can sit back and analyze. Then you got it made.
(He goes out. Only ANTOINETTE *and* MARY MUSHALKO *remain.)*

ANTOINETTE: You know, if you go to the fields in Poland, before they cut the hay, you almost always see a daisy. And the bluebells, and the lilies, and sometime when the spring comin', the forget-me-nots. They grow like this. And violets. You know that smell you get sometimes in some perfumes—they grow wild up there. And these people just go and pick them up and they make their own sachas, you know. In my country, you know, the good dirt is six feet down. Here in this country, maybe six inches. *(As lights dim out on image of* ANTOINETTE *and* MARY MUSHALKO *sitting at empty picnic table,* ANTOINETTE *hums an old Polish lullaby. Darkness.)*

(END)

Note on Sources

Note on Sources

Act 1. Steel and the City

SCENE 1   What makes a city? An official proclamation, a commitment to the common good, a vision of the future? It was typical that even as the elegant, transplanted Philadelphian Hugh Henry Brackenridge was correctly predicting for the town a great manufacturing future, scalping knives were still being sold in a local store. The dialogue for the scene is drawn largely from *Pittsburgh Gazette* notices and advertisements; Brackenridge's writings for the *Gazette*,[1] and the *Recollections* of his son;[2] and visitors' accounts of Pittsburgh, including those of Dr. Johann David Schoepf[3] and the traveler Anne Royall.[4]

SCENE 2   Just about the time Pittsburgh was incorporated into a borough, the "Whiskey Rebellion" (1794) presented the infant town with the first of many populist revolts that had to be quelled by outside forces. Leland Baldwin's *Whiskey Rebels*[5] was a useful source. A traditional song with new verses tells the story, which presages the strikes of subsequent years. A quarter of a century later, the rustic vigor of the whiskey rebels looked like ancient history.

SCENE 3   Pittsburgh had become the Iron City, a process of development we suggest through the words of citizens (notably the almanacker Zadok Cramer,[6] who published regularly in the period) and more visitors, including the actor Tyrone Power.[7] We also used Charles Dahlinger's *Pittsburgh, A Sketch of its Early Social Life*.[8]

SCENE 4   The War of 1812 demanded greater production from the city's mills; keel boats supplanted by steam boats carried iron goods in all directions.

SCENE 5   Only occasionally, as for the visit of the old war hero Lafayette, did the city suspend its business for a somewhat awkward bow to cosmopolitanism. The visit is well documented, the speeches and toasts recorded verbatim in the *Gazette*. We also drew on an article by Dahlinger in the July 1925 *Western Pennsylvania Historical Magazine*.[9]

SCENE 6   By mid-century, Pittsburgh was already a city of immigrants with the attendant problems, including a bigoted mayor actually elected while in jail. The transcript of Mayor Joe Barker's trial, newspaper accounts in the *Gazette*, records of the Sisters of Mercy,[10] and notorious Know-Nothing speeches of the era provided our dialogue. *Our Police* by Henry Mann[11] was especially useful. In the midst of the turmoil over Barker came an early ironworkers' strike, and the city (along with many other places in the world at this time) teetered on the brink of anarchy.

SCENE 7   About the same time there had settled in Pittsburgh a Scottish immigrant who, during the next fifty years would carry the city and himself to a peak of prosperity. Andrew Carnegie is so multifaceted a figure that we have chosen to put three of him in this scene, the primary sources for which were Carnegie's *Autobiography*[12] and *A Carnegie Anthology* arranged by Margaret Barclay Wilson.[13] The *Pittsburgh Gazette* for 2 November 1849 reports Carnegie's finding of the bank draft; we used it verbatim. Carnegie always seemed to be at the right place at the right time with the right amount of money. He also had a vision which shaped Pittsburgh's future; he understood that the new technology of Bessemer and the vast, developing frontier would together create the supply and demand for a great amount of steel. Our account of William Kelly's claim is taken from Boucher's *True History of the So-Called Bessemer Process*.[14] The opening of the Edgar Thomson works in 1875 marks the end of one era and the start of another. It cues in our play a Centennial tableau derived from America, a historical pageant by Pittsburgh's famous playwright of the time, Bartley Campbell.[15]

Act 2. Steel vs. the City

Just as our first act was based loosely on the form of a romantic epic, the melodrama—so popular in the 1880s and 1890s—proved useful to our conception of the second act. Toward the end of the act, as the action approaches the twentieth century, we drew upon images from early silent film, including the Keystone Cops and D. W. Griffith.

SCENE 1   The wedded fortunes of steel and the city had previously resembled a marriage of convenience; but in the last quarter of the nineteenth century an industry and a people often stood in bitter, hardened opposition. Steel consumed great quantities of men in twelve- and fourteen-hour days, which made their working lives resemble slavery. "Bessemer Parties" (a custom chronicled in the *Social Mirror* of the 1880s)[16] bespoke a widening gulf between the rich and the poor; even a sensitive soul like Elizabeth Moorhead, from whose charming autobiography (*Whirling Spindle*)[17] some of the scene's dialogue originates, averted her eyes from the appalling conditions which spawned the city's wealth.

SCENE 2   Throughout the period citizens seemed to be grouping in opposing forces, suggesting to us the recurring image of people banding together. The idea to present Carnegie's corporate organization as his bandwagon came from J. H. Bridge's *The Inside History of the Carnegie Steel Company*.[18]

SCENE 3   We also excerpted parts of the initiation ceremony of the Amalgamated Association of Iron, Steel and Tin Workers of America (founded in Pittsburgh in 1876).

SCENE 4   James J. Davis's *The Iron Puddler*[19] inspired our scene in the Greasy Spoon.

SCENE 5   A group of laborers entertain themselves on the South Side, until very recently a sanctum for the weary steelworker. The song "Soho on Saturday Night" was found in George Swetnam's *Where Else but Pittsburgh!*[20]

SCENE 6   The festivities are cut short by reports of a management ultimatum that threatens their livelihood.

SCENE 7   What happens when Carnegie's bandwagon, now led by the dynamic Henry Clay Frick, meets a mass of men joined in a union? Strikes—a number of them during the 1880s, as the Amalgamated grew in strength, culminating in the Homestead Strike of 1892. The issues were old ones: union recognition and a management attempt at reducing wages based on a sliding scale. Our rendition of the strike is compiled from contemporary newspaper accounts, as well as secondary sources ranging from *Henry Clay Frick the Man* by George Harvey[21] and *The Incredible Carnegie* by John Kennedy Winkler[22] to *Rebel in Paradise: A Biography of Emma Goldmann* by Richard Drinnon[23] and *Lockout* by Leon Wolff.[24] The strike song, like many in our play, may be found in *Pennsylvania Songs and Legends*.[25]

SCENE 8   Far from this arena of battle, almost in another world, are the gentlemen of this scene. Carnegie and the philosopher Herbert Spencer were friends; Russell Conwell, whose famous "Acres of Diamonds" sermon[26] was as popular in Pittsburgh as elsewhere, did not know the other two. So the scene we created never took place. But their collective eloquence—taken verbatim from their writings, including Carnegie's *Gospel of Wealth*[27] and Spencer's *Principles of Sociology*[28]—reveals the weight of social, religious, and philosophical opprobrium laid upon the poor.

SCENE 9   Among the rich, the news of the late nineties was of a scandalous quarrel between corporate titans. Carnegie and Frick settled out of court only when it became evident that their dispute was calling undue attention to questionable practices that allowed their enterprises to thrive.

SCENE 10   The scene, depicting the consolidation of United States Steel, was composed from Carnegie Steel Board meeting minutes and more than a dozen (often conflicting) accounts of the foundation of the first billion-dollar corporation. Biographers of Carnegie,[29] Frick,[30] Gary,[31] Schwab,[32] and Morgan[33] have all been at pains to turn their subjects into heroes or villains—a tendency that influenced our treatment of the material. In this era a yawning gap opened up between the magnates of industry and their largely immigrant work force caught in a kind of megamachine. Our closing images projected the Fifth Avenue mansions of the new millionaires and the slum housing on Pittsburgh hillsides as highly contrasting encampments in a city virtually divided against itself.

Act 3. Steel/City

The third act is a theatrical testament to an accommodation made between steel and the people of the city. Set in 1975 at a pensioners' picnic of a local steel company, it was composed primarily from the reminiscences of the workers

110 / Note on Sources

and their spouses recorded by our researchers and from oral histories in other collections, including those at the University of Pittsburgh,[34] the United Steelworkers of America Oral History Project at the Pennsylvania State University's Labor Archives,[35] and in the oral history archives of the Pennsylvania Historical and Museum Commission in Harrisburg.[36] Thus, not all of the people whose words we have used were at the picnic; but they belong together by virtue of common experience.

From the picnic we flash back to a scene of immigrant arrivals at the railroad station; to a boardinghouse typically crowded with hard-working men and the hard-working women who served them; and to the 1919 strike, our account of which is taken from newspaper reports, the writings of the organizer William Z. Foster,[37] Mary Marvin Vorse's *Men and Steel*,[38] and a voluminous study conducted by the Interchurch World Movement.[39] These people of Pittsburgh and environs—for *Steel/City* extends beyond the city limits—speak of pride in their work and in their ethnic heritage. They talk vigorously of the beliefs which sustained them through hard times and carried them through to happier times. They talk about the steel industry which, like a magnet gathering iron filings, drew their ancestors here to give Pittsburgh its rich, dense ethnic variety. They recall the need for banding together and staying together in the struggle for their rights. For them history is something alive, a source of passionate interest, not quaint and distant, but an invigorating part of the present.

We remember especially from the picnic Sam Davich, its organizer for many years. The picnic took place on a farm south of the city, owned by a steelworker from Slovakia who had bought it because it reminded him of the old country. Sam was in his seventies when we met him, feeling a little deflated because, following his fourth heart attack, he was going to have to give up smoking. Like all of the individuals we interviewed, Sam was invited to the opening night of *Steel/City*. Eager to get his reactions, we tracked him down in the lobby after the first act and asked him how he liked the show. His hands searched aimlessly for a cigarette that wasn't there. "It's O.K." We think he was being polite. After the second act, we checked in again with him. Warming to the union sympathies evident in act 2, he was more positive. But after the third act, he was glowing. He couldn't stop shaking our hands. Well, we wondered, were we going to be invited back to the picnic next year. "No," he replied. "The old man who owns the farm, he's too sick to have the picnic and his wife says it's too much work. There isn't going to be any more picnic. But that's all right," Sam smiled at us. "The picnic, it's there, on the stage, and it will be there forever."

Notes

1. Hugh Henry Brackenridge, *Gazette Publications by H. H. Brackenridge* (Carlisle, Pa.: Alexander & Phillips, 1806); Daniel Marder, ed., *A Hugh Henry Brackenridge Reader, 1770–1815* (Pittsburgh: University of Pittsburgh Press, 1970).

2. Henry Marie Brackenridge, *Recollections of Persons and Places in the West* (Pittsburgh, J. I. Kay, 1834; enl. ed. Philadelphia: Lippincott, 1868).

3. Johann David Schoepf, *The Climate and Diseases of America* (New York: Hurd and Houghton, 1875).

4. Anne Newport Royall, *Mrs. Royall's Pennsylvania, or, Travels Continued in the United States* (Washington, D.C.: published by the author, 1829).

5. Leland D. Baldwin, *Whiskey Rebels: The Story of a Frontier Uprising* (Pittsburgh: University of Pittsburgh Press, 1968).

6. See Zadok Cramer, *Cramer's Magazine Almanack* (Pittsburgh: Cramer and Spear). We consulted various volumes between 1803 and 1827.

7. Tyrone Power, *Impressions of America During the Years 1833, 1834, and 1835* (London: Richard Bentley, 1836).

8. Charles W. Dahlinger, *Pittsburgh, A Sketch of its Early Social Life* (New York: G. P. Putnam's Sons, 1916).

9. Charles W. Dahlinger, "General Lafayette's Visit to Pittsburgh in 1825," *Western Pennsylvania Historical Magazine* 8, no. 3 (July 1925).

10. Kathleen Healy, *Frances Warde: American Founder of the Sisters of Mercy* (New York: Seabury Press, 1973).

11. Henry Mann, ed., *Our Police: A History of the Pittsburgh Police Force, Under the Town and City* (Pittsburgh: 1889).

12. Andrew Carnegie, *Autobiography* (Boston: Houghton Mifflin, 1920).

13. Margaret Barclay Wilson, ed., *A Carnegie Anthology* (New York: privately printed, 1915).

14. John N. Boucher, *William Kelly: A True History of the So-Called Bessemer Process* (Greensburg, Pa.: published by the author, 1924); Herbert N. Casson, *The Romance of Steel: The Story of a Thousand Millionaires* (New York: Barnes, 1907).

15. Wayne Henry Claeken, "Bartley Campbell, Playwright of the Gilded Age," Ph.D. diss., University of Pittsburgh, 1975.

16. Adelaide Meillier Nevin, *Social Mirror: A Character Sketch of the Women of Pittsburg and Vicinity During the First Century of the Country's Existence* (Pittsburgh: T. W. Nevin, 1888).

17. Elizabeth Moorhead [Vermorcken], *Whirling Spindle: The Story of a Pittsburgh Family* (Pittsburgh: University of Pittsburgh Press, 1942).

18. James Howard Bridge, *The Inside History of the Carnegie Steel Company: A Romance of Millions* (1903; rpt. Pittsburgh: University of Pittsburgh Press, 1991).

19. James J. Davis, *The Iron Puddler: My Life in the Rolling Mills and What Came of It* (Indianapolis: Bobbs-Merrill, 1922).

20. George Swetnam, *Where Else but Pittsburgh!* (Pittsburgh: Davis & Warde, 1958).

21. George Harvey, *Henry Clay Frick the Man* (New York: Scribner's, 1928).

22. John Kennedy Winkler, *The Incredible Carnegie: The Life of Andrew Carnegie (1835–1919)* (New York: Vanguard, 1931).

23. Richard Drinnon, *Rebel in Paradise: A Biography of Emma Goldmann* (Chicago: University of Chicago Press, 1961).

24. Leon Wolff, *Lockout: The Story of the Homestead Strike of 1892; A Study of Violence, Unionism and the Carnegie Steel Empire* (New York: Harper & Row, 1965).

25. George Korson, ed. *Pennsylvania Songs and Legends* (Philadelphia: University of Pennsylvania Press, 1949).

26. Russell H. Conwell, *Acres of Diamonds* (New York and London: Harper, 1915).

27. Andrew Carnegie, *The Gospel of Wealth and Other Timely Essays* (New York: Century, 1900).

28. Herbert Spencer, *The Principles of Sociology* (D. Appleton, 1880–97; abr. ed., Hamden, Conn.: Archon, 1969).

29. Joseph Wall, *Andrew Carnegie* (New York: Oxford University Press, 1970).

30. George McClellan Harvey, *H. C. Frick, the Man* (New York: Scribner's 1928).

31. Ida Tarbell, *The Life of Elbert H. Gary: A Story of Steel* (1925; rpt. Westport, Conn.: Greenwood, 1969); see also Irving Sands Olds, *Judge Elbert H. Gary (1846–1927): His Life and Infuence upon American Industry* (New York: Newcomen Society, 1947).

32. Robert Hessen, *Steel Titan: The Life of Charles M. Schwab* (New York: Oxford University Press, 1975); Eugene G. Grace, *Charles M. Schwab* (Bethelehem, Pa., 1947).

33. Edwin Hoyt, Jr., *The House of Morgan* (New York: Dodd, Mead, 1966); Lewis Corey, *The House of Morgan: A Social Biography of the Masters of Money* (New York: AMS Press, 1969).

34. Homestead Album Oral History Project, 1976–77, 31 cassettes, conducted by the Pennsylvania Ethnic Heritage Studies Center, University of Pittsburgh; the Stanton Belfour Oral History Collection, 110 cassettes, with transcripts of interviews with individuals connected with post–World War II Pittsburgh redevelopment, Archives of Industrial Society, Hillman Library, University of Pittsburgh.

35. United Steelworkers of America Oral History Project, Pattee Library Collections, Pennsylvania State University.

36. Monessen Project, Manuscript Group #409, Oral History Collection, Pennsylvania Historical and Museum Commission, Harrisburg.

37. William Z. Foster, *American Trade Unionism: Principles and Organization, Strategy and Tactics; Selected Writings by W. Z. Foster* (New York: International Publishers, 1947).

38. Mary Marvin Vorse, *Men and Steel* (New York: Boni and Liveright, 1920).

39. Interchurch World Movement of North America, *Report on the Steel Strike of 1919, by the Commission of Inquiry, the Interchurch World Movement, Bishop Francis J. McConnell, Chairman . . . with the Technical Assistance of the Bureau of Industrial Research* (New York, Harcourt, Brace, and Howe, 1920); see also *Public Opinion and the Steel Strike: Supplementary Reports* (New York: Harcourt, Brace, 1921).